WHEN THE ANSWER IS NO!!!

A WIDOWER'S JOURNEY THROUGH GRIEF

MICHAEL REX BLAKELY

WHEN THE ANSWER IS NO!!!
Copyright © 2023 by Michael Rex Blakely

This publication contains the opinions and ideas of its author. It is intended to provide helpful and informative material on the subjects addressed in the publication. The authors and publisher specically ly disclaim all responsibility for any liability, loss, or risk, personal or otherwise, which is incurred as a consequence, directly or indirectly, of the use and application of any of the contents of this book.

ISBN:
      Paperback   979-8-88862-120-2
      Ebook   979-8-88862-126-4

DEDICATION/ACKNOWLEDGEMENTS

I would like to dedicate this book in honor and memory of my late wife Mary, whose will to live in the most adverse of situations continues to encourage me to this very day. I will always miss you!!!

Special thanks and acknowledgement go out to my current wife, Lisa, my son, Michael and my daughter, Sara. The way in which you choose to move forward in life despite the loss of parents encourages me to no end. I love ya'll bunches n bunches n bun!!!

Finally, I would like to thank my Heavenly Father. Without Him, Satan would have sifted through me like fine wheat years ago. Thank you, Lord, for showing yourself strongest in my broken places!!!

TABLE OF CONTENTS

CHAPTER ONE
ULTRASOUND

The pain Mary had been experiencing in the small of her back had gradually increased from tolerable to excruciating. She had been dealing with back pain since being involved in a head-on auto collision during the summer of 1992. Fast forward 25 years to the summer of 2017 and this level of pain was entirely different! It started in the small of her back, began to spread to her sides and occasionally worked its way into her abdominal cavity. She knew that it was time to make an appointment with her primary care physician.

August 28, 2017 at 11 a.m. was the date and time for Mary's appointment with her physician. That morning started like so many other mornings during our 35 plus years of marriage. We would each do our individual devotionals and then discuss any particular scripture that inspired us before joining together in prayer. That morning we specifically prayed (Isaiah 53:5 NKJV) that by Jesus' stripes Mary would receive her healing. That whatever was causing the pain would be removed and the pain eliminated in Jesus's name! We had no reason to believe otherwise since God had previously healed both our backs and had answered numerous prayer requests to our satisfaction. Besides, by God's grace and the measure of faith imparted to us by His Spirit to receive Jesus Christ as our Lord and Saviour, surely nothing of any significance would be allowed to penetrate the hedge of protection that God had surrounding us!

As we drove closer to the physician's office, Mary became somewhat apprehensive, as was to be expected, since this level and type of pain was new to her. However, she was very comfortable with her physician since she had been a patient of hers for a number of years. By the time we arrived for the appointment, Mary's pain began to intensify instead of dissipating as we had prayed for. Mary's physician immediately recognized the amount of pain and discomfort that she was in which prompted her to administer pain meds immediately.

Mary complied without hesitancy which is a very rare thing for her. You see, Mary's the type of person that would hardly ever take a Tylenol much less prescribed pain medication. For this reason, I, Mickey, her husband for 35 plus years started to become very concerned and developed that feeling in the pit of my stomach that no one wants to experience. I knew in that moment that our faith would be tested as never before in this fallen world in which we live.

After the pain meds started to kick in and Mary became more comfortable, her physician determined that she needed to perform an ultrasound of Mary's back, sides and abdominal cavity. The results concluded that her back and sides were fine but there appeared to be multiple cysts in her abdominal cavity. Because of these results, Mary's physician set up an appointment for both a colonoscopy and an endoscopy with a local GI physician on September 8, 2017 at 1 p.m.

Upon leaving the doctor's office and driving home, we began to discuss the results of the ultrasound. Mary was somewhat upset with herself for not having a colonoscopy when she had turned 60 almost 3 years earlier. I felt led to comfort her by saying that we have no idea what we're really dealing with, besides even if we did it wouldn't change anything. So, let's not speculate on the what if's, that'll just twist our stomachs into more knots than are already there. She agreed, from that point forward we promised each other to be real in the moments that we would face together as we received more in-depth test results. In this moment, we were both very concerned with the level of pain that she was in!

We pretty much carried on with our lives the rest of the week like we always do. We both have elderly parents whom both live out of town that we visit on a weekly basis. Labor Day weekend we visited her mom on Saturday and my parents that Sunday. Mary's mother had been widowed for a number of years and struggled with some health issues that prevented her from driving. So, it was typical to shop for groceries, do laundry and run other errands when we would visit. Mary along with her sister were her mom's power of attorney. Mary's sister lived out of town so the brunt of responsibility fell into Mary's lap.

My parents were both healthy so on the most part when we visit it is strictly to visit. Per usual, Mary being Mary would go in, say hello and then leave to go shopping to be amongst the people. This arrangement worked well for us since I'm the ultimate homebody and this allowed me to spend quality time with my parents. Most of the time Mary would bring something back to eat for supper. She and my parents got along great and loved each other unconditionally. Who knew this would be the last time that they would see one another.

During this timeframe no matter how hard you try, you can't help but find yourself thinking what if this is something really bad! I know, I'm already breaking a promise but I'm just being real! In those moments I would find myself singing in my mind & holding onto 2 Corinthians 10:5 (KJV) "casting down imaginations, and every high thing that exalteth itself against the knowledge of God, bringing into captivity every thought to the obedience of Christ". I had fortunately memorized this verse over three decades earlier with the assistance from a Christian group at church who had written and would perform a song with this verse word for word. God was already bringing His word to my remembrance as I needed it to sustain me. We truly serve an awesome God!

CHAPTER TWO
EMERGENCY ROOM

It was Labor Day afternoon exactly one week since Mary had her visit with her physician. The pain meds along with heavy doses of prayer had been keeping the pain in Mary's abdomen at bay. Until now, it was evident that she wasn't doing very well. I asked if she wanted to go to the ER but she declined, she just wanted to eat some oatmeal, toast, take medicine and lay down. I honored her request.

After Mary went to sleep, I went outside and started to cut grass. We had a little over an acre and it would take me about an hour and a half to mow. It may sound crazy but I have some of my best talks with the Lord when I'm cutting grass. I had just finished with the front yard and had moved around back when I noticed Mary coming out the back door. I immediately stopped and went up to the house. She was doubled over in pain so I helped her into the SUV and drove her to the local ER. My conversation with the Lord would have to continue later.

Upon arriving at the ER and after being checked-in, the nurse asked the standard questions while taking Mary's vitals. Fortunately, shortly thereafter the physicians' assistant arrived and proceeded to ask follow-up questions regarding the source of Mary's pain and the ultrasound performed at the previous weeks' office visit.

The physician's assistant then ordered an IV to be started immediately to both rehydrate and provide medications to treat Mary's pain and nausea. She then ordered a CT scan to get a more in-depth look at what was causing the pain, cramping & nausea originating from Mary's abdominal cavity. A few minutes later they rolled Mary out to radiology for the CT scan. The technician stated that they would have her back in a couple of hours or so.

I went to the vending area to get some coffee and to try to wrap my head around what was happening. Suddenly, things with Mary were happening at a more rapid pace than I was anticipating and she later acknowledged the same. I went back to Mary's room to wait for her return and eventually the results of the CT scan. When she returned to the room, Mary was on cloud nine. It was evident that the medications administered to her were working properly. She was smiling, laughing and engaging in conversation which is who she is. It is a moment that I will cherish forever!

While waiting for the results of the CT scan we started to watch the UT Vols football game. They were playing GA Tech in the Chick-fil-A Kickoff game at Mercedes Benz Stadium in Atlanta GA. This was somewhat common ground for the two of us. I love to watch college football, especially UT Vols football and Mary would enjoy the excitement aspect of football for a period of time until it was time to go shopping, her favorite pastime. We were both enjoying ourselves especially considering the circumstances until the physicians' assistant returned with the CT scan results and she immediately turned the tv off.

She proceeded to inform us that the results indicate a worst-case diagnosis. That there is a tumor in your abdominal cavity that appears to have spread to your liver and possibly to a lymph node above the liver. That Mary would need to undergo further testing to confirm this diagnosis. Her preliminary diagnosis is that Mary has terminal stage 4 cancer and needs to see an oncologist immediately. Since Mary already had an appointment scheduled in four days with a gastro-intestinal specialist, she referred Mary to an oncologist and prescribed her a proper amount of pain and nausea meds before discharging her.

At that point I walked out to the parking lot to get the SUV, my mind was all over the place. While waiting for the nurse to wheelchair Mary out I remember thinking out loud, "surely this can't be happening, especially not to my Mary". In my mind I started conversing with God, this makes no sense! How can this be! Mary's the most diligent person that I know when it comes to spending time with you in your word and praying for people! The majority of the time thinking about and doing for others before herself! At that moment the nurse who had been assigned to Mary was bringing her out.

The nurse who was assigned to Mary was in her early to mid-twenties. She pretty much befriended Mary immediately, spending as much time with her as possible without relinquishing her other duties. I believe that she saw Mary as a mother figure. Whatever the reason, she had prayed with Mary during her stay and later would give Mary an inspirational handbook which had help to inspire her during some difficult times in her life. This is an example of what would become typical throughout Mary's journey within the medical community. God always seemed to have someone in place to step up and provide comfort especially during those moments when it was most needed.

Once getting Mary in the car and leaving the ER, the conversation that neither of us could have ever imagine having begun. It turned out to be short, powerful and to the point. It started with her asking me what I thought about all that had happened tonight. I responded, it's a lot! I'm just trying to stay in the moment as we promised and process it by talking to the Lord about it. Mary said that she was doing the same. We then joined hands and prayed Isaiah 53:5 (KJV), "but He was wounded for our transgressions, He was bruised for our iniquities; the chastisement of our peace was upon Him; and with His stripes we are healed!"

After praying we then drove to Kroger to pick up some items for Mary's new diet. Soft foods such as soups, jello, pudding, ice cream and ensure. While walking through the aisles of the store she had a calmness and a peace about her that had been missing for a couple of weeks. I asked her about it expressing that I noticed something different about her for the better. She said that this was the first time in the past two weeks that she was without pain. She felt that she was normal again and could live the way that she enjoyed living. This was such a blessing to hear! Thank you, Jesus!

Once arriving home, Mary went straight to bed. She literally was feeling no pain and was looking forward to a good night's rest. I went to the rec room which is on the opposite end of the house from the bedrooms and tried to watch some TV. It seemed that no matter which channel I surfed to there was a commercial about some form of cancer treatment. It's funny how you pay no attention to certain things until it becomes relevant to your life and it hits close to home. It was at that moment that I started to entertain the reality that Mary could really have stage 4 cancer. No matter how hard I tried to cast that thought down, I could hear the voice of the physicians' assistant echoing in my mind, "the two of you have a long, hard road ahead of you."

I started to panic, I went outside and walked around our property talking to the Lord just trying to compose myself. By this this time it was around midnight and was getting a little chilly outside. I then sat inside our Dodge Intrepid that we parked outside and just sobbed, cried and let out all the emotion that had been pent up inside of me after hearing the preliminary diagnosis. I had this feeling in the pit of my stomach that this was not going to turn out the way that I wanted it to no matter how I prayed for a different outcome. The Lord confirmed this in my spirit but encouraged me to stay in communion with Him, to continue to stand on His word and to walk by faith not by sight. While this gave me some peace and comfort it didn't give me any understanding. I was beginning to realize that when God withholds information from us it's for our benefit. He wants this withholding to draw us closer to Him which in turn guards and protects both our hearts and our minds. (Philippians 4:6 KJV, "and the peace that surpasses all understanding will guard your hearts and minds in Christ Jesus." Isaiah 55:8-9 KJV, "for my thoughts are not your thoughts, neither are your ways my ways, saith the Lord. For as the heavens are higher than the earth, so are my ways higher than your ways, and my thoughts than your thoughts.")

To conclude this life changing day, I snuggled in close to my wife and held her like I have never held her before. By God's grace, we both were blessed with a very lengthy and peaceful night's rest! The remainder of the week was fairly typical with the one exception being that Mary was more of a homebody than usual. She seemed more content to relax at home and read for the most part of the day. She loved to read! Her appetite was off due to her condition but I was very thankful that she ate enough to stomach her medications.

This would be the case until the day before her scheduled endoscopy and colonoscopy. This was the day she had to prep for these procedures by drinking a solution that would flush your system out. Unfortunately for Mary, this process severely agitated her stomach to the point that she couldn't keep her meds down. This caused the pain to return along with severe headaches and nauseousness. This would be the first of many similar nights that we would face together. We both slept very little that night but by God's grace we were up at the crack of dawn and headed to the gastrointestinal doctor's office for the procedures to be performed.

CHAPTER THREE
COLONOSCOPY AND ENDOSCOPY

It was September 12, 2017 at 7 a.m. when we arrived at the medical facility. A mere fifteen days since Mary's appointment with her primary care physician. Mary was promptly admitted and assigned a locker to place her clothing after undressing into the gown provided. The hospital staff allowed me to stay with her until they actually rolled her back to have the procedures performed. During this time, the nurse asked the standard questions, took her vitals and started an IV to administer the necessary medications. Once the medications kicked in, Mary was once again her usual, glowing self because she was feeling no pain or nauseousness. We then prayed for guidance and wisdom for the physician and her staff in addition for peace and comfort for Mary while the procedures were being performed. Most importantly we were praying for a good report! It was very comforting and such a blessing to see Mary rolled away with a smile on her face. It was then time for me to proceed to the waiting area until further notified.

To me, I find the waiting area as a very humbling and grounding place to be; especially one inside a specialized medical facility like the one I found myself presently sitting in. It's an opportunity to connect with people who are all having a similar experience in life. In this case there were five of us who were all waiting for spouses who were having the same procedure or procedures performed. Two were there due to meeting the appropriate age requirement but three, including Mary, were having the procedures due to some kind of gastrointestinal issues. As you might expect, the three of us who had spouses with these issues began to engage in conversation.

I'm not a very social person at all, but there have been many times throughout my life where social engagement unfortunately has been required but then again sometimes welcomed. This is one of those times that it was welcomed! The three of us each shared the individual journey that each of our spouses had endured to arrive at this point. This was new territory for each one of us. I shared now I know how it feels for the shoe to be on the other foot. I had an uncle on my mothers' side who passed due to colon cancer in his 50's. This initiated me having colonoscopies for the past 20 plus years. So, my wife had worn this shoe several times throughout our 35 years of marriage. Thankfully, the physician found only benign polyps each time and they were easily removed during the procedure. We were all hoping that this would be the case with each our spouses. I was about to find out about Mary because they just called me back.

It was good to be back at Mary's side. She was still smiling and pain free due to the effects of the anesthesia. Thank God for anesthesia and pain management! Could you imagine the pain and suffering we humans would have to endure if God had not created the essential elements and provided the knowledge and wisdom to mankind to produce medicines that assist in the healing of our bodies! Praise be to God in the highest for His goodness! Mary and I both were rejoicing for this heavenly moment that we were experiencing and both were thanking Him in advance for a good report. We were about to find out with the nurse assisting on the procedures just having entered the room.

I was very familiar and surprisingly somewhat comfortable being on this side of the process as opposed to the waiting area. That's mainly because all of my previous experiences had resulted in a good report. The difference this time being that the procedures in this case were performed on my wife who was here as the result of pain manifesting in her abdominal cavity. Mary and I held hands and braced ourselves as the nurse began to brief us on the results of the colonoscopy. With pictures in hand, he reported that Mary had the healthiest and best-looking colon that he had ever laid eyes on! This prompted us to laugh out loud as we both breathed a big sigh of relief. Mary thanked the Lord out loud as a heavy load of guilt was instantaneously removed from her mind. She had carried this guilt around since her preliminary diagnosis because she had failed to get a colonoscopy almost 3 years earlier at the age of 60. Our celebration would be brief as the nurse then informed us that the physician specialist would be in shortly to discuss the results of the endoscopy.

As soon as the nurse retreated, Mary gripping my hand tightly, stated that this means the second report has to be bad news. I responded, not necessarily! While I agree that the report isn't going to be as straight forward as the first or the nurse would have given us both reports simultaneously. It's been my experience over the past 20 plus years that unless the physician had to remove polyps or stretch my esophagus, I received a clean bill of health from the nurse and was discharged. So, it's possible that the physician was able to remove the obstruction which was causing the pain. I think that we both would agree that that would be a good report. Let's not jump to any conclusions good or bad and just hold each other until the GI physician arrives.

Mary's GI physician presented as a very professional but yet sincere and compassionate woman. There was a calmness about her that carried over into the presentation of the results of the endoscopy. This calmness set the tone for Mary and I to receive the results with an open mindedness and an understanding for such a time as this. She proceeded to tell us that she was able to perform a complete endoscopy examination until she reached the central part of the duodenum which is the first part of the small intestine. The examined area which included the esophagus, stomach and first part of the duodenum were in perfect working condition. Now, for the concerning aspect of the report.

She stated that Mary's duodenum was about 80% restricted. Due to this restriction, she was unable to collect a sample of tissue beyond this point to biopsy and determine whether the obstruction was benign or malignant. This obstruction in conjunction with the

restriction were the root cause or the source of pain that Mary was experiencing. She believed that it would be best to prepare for the worse and hope for the best. Based on this recommendation, she had already scheduled appointments with an oncologist
on September 22, 2017 and with an abdominal surgeon on October 2, 2017. She assured us that if she were in Mary's shoes, these two medical professionals would be the ones that she would want attending to her. She also encouraged us to get away if possible and enjoy the things that the two of you enjoy doing. She stated how we have 10 days until the next appointment so take advantage of it. While this sounded exciting, honestly it came across as somewhat unsettling.

CHAPTER FOUR
BILOXI MS TRIP

It has been 4 days since Mary's appointment with her GI doctor. Since then, I keep mulling over in my mind the words that she spoke as we were leaving the medical facility. That we needed to get away if possible and do the things that we enjoy. It just so happened that we had been planning a 3 day get away with one of our closest couple friends to go to Biloxi MS. Mary and I kept going back and forth on how she would do on such a trip. It was about an 8-hour drive one way from where we lived plus the stomach issues were not conducive for her to do well riding in a vehicle for that length of time. We really wanted to go because not only do we love the beautiful views on the gulf coast but thoroughly enjoy the types of delicious seafood available. After much prayer and thought, we decided that we would go. Mary had felt relatively well these past 4 days since her stomach had a chance to settle down from all the manipulation caused by the scoping's. Our main concern was the traveling, so our plan was for her to medicate enough to lay down and sleep in the back seat for the majority of the drive down. We then called our friends to confirm that we were going. They were excited and told us to be ready to be picked up at 8 the next morning if that worked for us.

The trip down to Biloxi was peaceful and calming. Mary pretty much slept or rested the majority of the ride down. We arrived at the hotel around supper time and after checking in, we departed to go eat supper at the Half Shell Oyster House located down the street from the hotel. Our friends had dined there several times before but it would be our first time there. Mary loved crab legs, lobster, shrimp and catfish but her appetite was not on board with the seafood section of the menu. She opted to have a BLT, hold the mayo and had it served open faced. It was a blessing to see her eat something other than soft foods for a change. It's moments like these that you hold on to. It's moments like these that help sustain, encourage and give you hope to endure each day. Even though she never expressed this, I know that she wanted to eat seafood so badly. I was so proud of her for exercising wisdom.

After leaving the restaurant, we drove along enjoying the views of the gulf coast. Mary was feeling well enough to sit up and enjoy the sun glimmering on the emerald waters as it began to disappear over the horizon. While driving back to the hotel, we discussed with our friends what the plans were for tomorrow. The women had a spa day planned, while the men would be playing golf or as in my case attempting to. Of course, this would be contingent upon how Mary felt the next day. Before retreating to our respective rooms, we all laid hands on Mary praying for her healing. Our friends are some praying people and it was very much appreciated and welcomed.

As Mary and I lay in bed that night, we both were as content as two people could possibly be considering the circumstances. We praised God for blessing us with the opportunity through our friends to get away as recommended by her GI physician. We praised Him for Mary being without pain and nauseousness on this trip. We praised Him for touching both of us to be in a sound and proper frame of mind to discuss truthfully how each one of us felt in this moment. Prior to this moment, things had transpired so fast that whether we both realized it or not, we both were overwhelmed, somewhat traumatized and in shock due to the nature of the preliminary diagnosis and the manifestations of such that were occurring in Mary's body. So, now we would have the conversation that you never want to have!

Even though Mary was the talker between the two of us, I felt impressed to begin this conversation. Mary smiled and said please because I'm just dying to hear what's going on in that analytical mind of yours. When we both realized what she had said, at first, it gave both of us chills but then we laughed it off shaking our heads. Mary had a heck of a sense of humor but in this case, she was being sincere. I began by saying that I couldn't believe that we would ever be having this conversation at this stage of our lives, and if we were, it would be because of me having health issues instead of her because of the longevity of life on her side of the family. Even though the preliminary diagnosis suggests that the activity is cancerous, there's no history of cancer on your side of the family and the women on both your mom's and dad's side live into their 90's with some living to be over 100 years of age.

So, this diagnosis has really knocked me for a loop and as off balance as I've ever been in my life. Honestly, I'm very scared. Ever since the ER visit after you go to sleep, I spend a lot of time talking with the Lord. I just lay it out there to Him! I know it's a preliminary diagnosis but I can sense in my spirit that this is how people die from cancer! Lord, I want to believe in your report that states that by Jesus' stripes that you're healed! That the name of Jesus is above all names which includes cancer and in the name of Jesus, cancer you are bound and cast out! That from the crown of your head to the soles of your feet that you may prosper and be in good health, just as your soul prospers! That if anyone is sick among you, call for the elders of the church to anoint them with oil in the name of the Lord and the prayer of faith will restore the one who is sick and the Lord will raise them up! I could go on and on but no matter how often I pray and stand on God's word my spirit concerning this diagnosis remains very unsettled and troubled. In fact, honey I found myself asking God, this is not going to turn out the way that I want it to, is it? He replied, no it's not! So, I don't know what that means but I know that I'm not ready to let you go or lose what we have because we're just getting started in retirement together. I promise to continue to love you, hold you, provide for you, pray for you and be for you whatever it is that you need me to be for you in Jesus' name, amen!

Mary grabbed ahold of me, held me and started sobbing like she never had before. I comforted her and told her just to let it out.

This was unlike Mary, she very rarely cried or outwardly expressed what would be considered a much-needed emotional release. She stated that my honesty had caught her off guard but that is what she wanted and needed to hear. She also stated that she was scared but that she also had an underlying peace that she couldn't explain. That while I thought she was sleeping some nights that she as well was having a heart to heart with our Heavenly Father. That she laid her heart's desire out to Him that she wasn't ready to die but that if that was His plan for her that in His timing, her faith told her that He would properly prepare her to submit to His will to transcend to her heavenly home. Then in true Mary being Mary fashion she stated like me not accepting God's plan is going to persuade Him to change His mind anyway, we both chuckled.

My reaction was "wow." In that moment, in spite of the seriousness of the conversation we both felt like a weight had been lifted off our shoulders. I believe that when we accept God's will for our lives, we relinquish the self-imposed responsibilities to where they properly belong which is in the hands of God! We both just started grinning and laughing. For the first time since this journey started. We were fully able to function as the married couple that we had been for over 35 years. Little did we know, this would be the last time!

After an awesome night's rest, we started getting ready for the day's activities. The ladies departed for their spa day while the guys headed to the golf course. While I didn't like being away from Mary, I was looking forward to spending some time with my friend out on the golf course. I was hoping and praying that we wouldn't be paired up with anyone else and that the course wouldn't be crowded. Both requests were granted. We were able to tee off immediately and pretty much had the course to ourselves. Both of us are mid handicappers at best and considering what was going on with Mary, I knew that it was going to be challenging to keep my head in the game. Golf is such a mental sport which requires a proper amount of thought and concentration. I was thankful to be playing with this particular friend. Typically, neither one of us takes our golf game that seriously if the wheels fall off plus we had played golf together for approximately 20 years. We had played on the big island of Hawaii, Kauai, California, Florida, Idaho, Kentucky, South Carolina, Tennessee, Washington State and now Mississippi.

My friend being a few years my senior, I always saw him as an older brother type in my life. I'm the oldest sibling of 5 children so he at times fulfilled that void. He's very grounded spiritually and was the perfect person to be playing golf with this day. We talked most of the time about family and I caught him up on what was going on with Mary. I told him how my spirit was troubled concerning Mary's healing and he said that all you can do is what you're doing which is to pray and stand on God's word. I agreed!

Concerning golf that day, we must have played fairly well. I only remember one bad hole for me that day. I had played a par 5 with 2 near perfect shots only leaving me with a 60-yard little pitch shot to the green and would be putting for birdie. Instead, I pushed the shot which plugged in the face of an 8-foot-deep bunker. It took me 4 shots to get out of the bunker plus 2 putts which resulted in a quadruple bogey 9. What should have been an easy par 5 turned into a quadruple bogey 9. Kind of a microcosm of life, you can be moving along quite nicely when suddenly you find yourself over your head in a circumstance that you never saw coming.

After we finished playing golf, we stopped and ate some lunch before heading back to the hotel. It's funny the things that you remember, on the way to lunch the gps took us to the middle of a subdivision instead of to the restaurant. What can I say, just one of those head scratching moments in life. After returning to the hotel, I immediately went to the room to check on Mary. She had had a somewhat pleasant day. She received most of the spa treatment package but just wasn't up for all of it. We both napped for a couple of hours before getting ready for supper. A couple from Louisiana who were mutual friends of ours were driving in to have supper with us that night.

The couple that was joining us that night are very special people to the four of us. He was one of the associate pastors at the church that we had attended for several years. He also was the principal of the Christian Academy that was affiliated with the church. Mary and I had children that were similar in age to theirs resulting in them attending school and children's church together. We also attended several activities outside of church together such as birthday parties, in-home bible studies, cookouts and other outdoor events. They had since moved back home to Louisiana after several years of ministry in Tennessee. They have an anointing upon their lives, their marriage and their ministry.

Mary and I were really looking forward to spending some time together with our friends that evening. Honestly, I don't remember what we had for supper that night or even much of the conversation but what I do remember is that Mary had a glow about her, a radiance that was emanating both around and from within her. After eating, she began speaking about the preliminary diagnosis and just pretty much catching our friends from Louisiana up on what we had been dealing with over the past 2-3 weeks and what we were facing appointment wise upon arriving back home. I was somewhat taken back by the calm, contented and peaceful manner in which the words were flowing out of her mouth while speaking. It was evident that God's anointing was resting upon her at this very moment. Before we departed to go our separate ways that night, we anointed Mary with oil with the laying on of hands and prayed for in particular that she would receive her healing. It was the perfect ending to a blessed time of fellowship with folks who are more family than friends.

After another awesome night's rest, we were packed up and ready for the ride back to Tennessee. Whereas Mary pretty much had to lay down on the trip down, she felt so well that she on the most part sat up on the trip back home. We were able to engage in conversation as we normally would. Upon arriving home, we thanked our friends so much for their generosity and fellowship. We all thanked God for His protection and other blessings provided on this trip which led to ending in prayer for Mary's healing and our friend's safe arrival home.

CHAPTER FIVE
ONCOLOGY

It was Sept. 22, 2017, 3 days after our return home from the Biloxi MS trip. Mary's daily routine was practically back to normal. The regimen that she had incorporated concerning prayer, diet and medication seemed to be working quite well. So, now we're off to the Oncologists office for her initial visit. It would be new territory for the both of us. Up to this point in our lives, cancer consultation and/or treatment had never hit so close to home. After parking at the facility, we joined in prayer for the Lord to provide guidance and wisdom to the Oncologist as pertaining to His will for Mary.

Mary's Oncologist was a very professional man with a pleasant and calming demeanor. He proceeded to tell us that he had read and looked over the reports provided to him from the previous attending physicians. He stated that there was a great cause for concern regarding the potential of possible cancer in Mary's duodenum and liver. He specifically emphasized possible cancer; we do not call it cancer until we have pathology that confirms a cancer diagnosis. Because of this, he wanted to perform a complete examination to rule out any potential lumps, moles or other outward signs of cancer and to establish Mary's overall physicality. After performing this examination, he ruled out any visible or outward signs of possible cancer and determined that Mary's overall physicality was great with the exception being the possible cancer. He stated that her overall health would play a vital role pertaining to her responding to treatment if treatment was necessary. This being Friday, he then scheduled appointments the following week for a liver biopsy on Tuesday Sept. 26, a PET scan on Thursday Sept. 28 and finally a follow-up visit to go over the results at his office on Friday Sept. 29.

Upon leaving the Oncologists office we were so very thankful that we took Mary's GI physicians advice and left town for a few days. We decided that we would go visit and check on her mother the next day since it had been 3 weeks since we had last visited. She made me promise not to tell her mom anything about what was going on even if this turned out to be worst case and Mary were to pass. At first, I didn't know what to make of this. I mean a mother has the right to know what's going on with her children. Right! Mary's reasoning for this decision was based on two previous experiences in which family members had opted to tell Mary's mom about the passing of both a grandson and a daughter-in-law. Mary's mom struggles with memory loss issues and has a current event memory of about 5-10 minutes. In essence, every 5-10 minutes she'll ask the same questions. So, if Mary were to die, she didn't want her mother reliving her passing every 5-10 minutes! Furthermore, Mary's mom had made the comment for years that her greatest fear of living so long was that if one of her children passed before her, she didn't know if she could survive that. Mary being her mom's primary care giver up to this point didn't want to put her mom in that situation by her knowing if she were to pass. Made sense to me!

The drive up to her mom's is about an hour and a half drive. It's a very pleasant, relaxing drive with the majority being on rural state highways. It's very scenic and picturesque with the longest part driving through valleys surrounded by the hills that are prevalent in Middle Tennessee. Mary and I always had some great conversations when driving to her mom's and also when driving to my parents for that matter. This particular day, we had no way of knowing that this would the last drive together to her mom's with   Mary being pain free and without any nausea. Upon arriving at her mom's, Mary reminded me to stay mum on what may be going on with her. I again promised that I wouldn't say a word.

Mary's mom was currently residing in an assisted living facility. She had been living here for almost 10 months since the beginning of the year. The staff here are amazing! They really take top notch care of the residents at their facility. The facility manager is very personable and has been a great resource for Mary and her family. For these reasons, Mary has been able to be more hands off these last few weeks due to her pressing medical issues which has been a blessing. We had a much-needed conversation with the facility manager to let her in on what was going on with Mary. She was taken aback, which was to be expected but assured us that she would stay in contact with us as much as was warranted. Mary also told her not to let her mom in on what is going on with her. She said that would not be an issue. The facility manager pulled me to the side and told me that she would take care of Mary's mom so you just focus on taking care of Mary. I told her that we thank God for you and what a blessing you have been to us these past almost 10 months.

As usual on our visits with Mary's mom, we would take her riding around to get her out of the facility for a while. She loved to get a chocolate milk shake and a grilled cheese from Sonic while we would drive a loop for about an hour around her old stomping grounds. It's amazing how even though she struggles with loss of memory issues, she could tell you everything that happened the last 50 plus years in detail at each location as we drove around. I really enjoyed listening to the stories and learning about Mary's family history. After returning Mary's mom home and getting her settled, Mary and I looked at each other realizing that there was a good chance that this may have been the last time that the two of us would take her mom riding. The ride back home was very sad with very little conversation. It's one of those moments that still troubles me to this very day.

Even though it was only Saturday night and Mary's liver biopsy wasn't scheduled until Tuesday, the round trip to Mary's moms had left us both physically, emotionally, mentally and spiritually drained. We were wiped out! So, instead of visiting my parents on Sunday like we normally would, we decided that it would be best if we just stayed home, relaxed and recharged our batteries in all areas until the appointment on Tuesday morning.

Mary had to fast to prepare for the liver biopsy which disrupted her daily regimen that had been working well for her. Because of this, she would be taking both pain and nausea medication on an empty stomach. Unfortunately, this prompted both pain and nausea to return. It was very disappointing considering the fact that she hadn't experienced either of these symptoms for a number of days. The liver biopsy procedure went very smoothly. Mary was given local anesthesia beforehand and we were back home within a couple of hours.

My primary concern at this time was to get some food into Mary's system which would hopefully calm her stomach and get her back on track experiencing no pain or nausea. She said that nothing sounded good to her and that she just wanted to lie down and rest. While Mary was resting, our friends that we traveled to Biloxi with called to check on her. I informed them while the biopsy went fine, Mary wasn't feeling well due to taking medication on an empty stomach and had no appetite. This information prompted them to prepare and bring over one of Mary's favorite meals, chicken tetrazzini.

When Mary had woke up, I informed her that we would be having company and they would be bringing one of her favorite meals. She was delighted to hear this especially when hearing who it was and that the meal would be chicken tetrazzini. We both erupted with laughter when both our stomachs started growling simultaneously. When our friends arrived, we immediately blessed the food and prayed that Mary would be able to eat well which would assist in her healing. Thankfully, she was able to stomach a good amount of food and able to take her meds without any issues. We fellowshipped for a bit and after our friends left, Mary and I retired for the evening.

It's now the morning of Sept. 28th, the day that Mary has a PET scan scheduled for 1:00 P.M. Unfortunately, she woke up this morning not feeling very well at all. She was both nauseous and in a good bit of pain. She was having trouble keeping anything down. I called the Oncologist to see if we could reschedule because we knew that she would have to drink two large glasses of contrast and we didn't believe that she would be capable of doing this much less holding it down. He replied that it was of the upmost importance that Mary have this PET scan done immediately to help determine what we were dealing with. He said that he would call ahead and have them meet us at the door and they would properly assist Mary in making this process as comfortable as possible.

Upon arriving at the Imaging Center, the staff were waiting for our arrival and promptly rolled Mary away to a private room. I proceeded to the check-in counter to fill out the necessary paperwork also providing the required credentials. They informed me that it would be a couple of hours before she would be discharged and that I could stay or leave. I decided to go sit in our SUV, try to relax and talk to the Lord. Not much conversation took place, evidently, I fell asleep awaking to the alarm that I had set on my phone. That two hours seemed more like twenty minutes. I immediately went inside and waited approximately 15-20 minutes for Mary to be discharged.

It was about a 20-30 minute ride home. It was evident that Mary wasn't feeling very well. As to be expected, she was only able to drink about half the contrast required but thankfully that was enough to obtain a proper scan. Once we arrived home, I got Mary washed up and she just wanted to go sleep. While she was sleeping, I called the oncology nurses hotline to ask some questions and to get a better understanding of what to do if Mary wasn't able to properly medicate due to her upchucking the medications. It would be the first of many such calls.

We have a pool table in our recreational room above our garage. Honestly, we never played much pool, instead it was typically used as a catch-all for various items. After Mary's first oncology visit, I had cleared it off to set-up shop for all the new medications prescribed by the Oncologist. I kept them separated by category of treatment tagged with post-it notes to remind me as to what dose and when to properly administer. After speaking with the nurse, I now had a new set of instructions which was to physically go through Mary's vomit to determine if she had kept any medication down or if it had to be readministered. It's amazing how God's grace is sufficient to do certain things in life that are required of us from time to time. Blood has never phased me but throw up usually gets me every time until now. You just find yourself doing what is necessary.

After an up and down night of somewhat resting, Mary and I headed to the medical facility for the follow-up visit with her Oncologist. It was obvious that Mary's condition unfortunately had regressed to the point of much pain and nausea. I attributed this to the manipulation of her stomach over the past 3 days resulting in her being unable to keep her meds down. Upon arrival, we joined with our son outside the facility before heading inside. He wanted to be there for support and to be kept in the loop on what was going on with his mom. Once inside, Mary's oncologist immediately recognized that her condition had declined from the previous visit prompting him to have his head nurse start an IV for Mary to receive the proper medications. Fortunately, the symptoms that she was experiencing were relieved in a matter of minutes. While Mary was resting and conversing with her new best friend (head nurse), her Oncologist led my son and I to a conference room which we thought would be to discuss and go over the results of her liver biopsy and PET scan.

Once inside the conference room, we were joined by the Oncologists PA (physician's assistant). He immediately stated that due to Mary's worsening condition, that he wanted his PA to have her admitted to the ER at their facility so that she could be transferred immediately to the Sarah Cannon Cancer Center at a sister facility in Nashville. His concern is that the restriction in her duodenum was getting worse and could warrant emergency surgery. He had already called ahead to speak with the attending surgeon on call for the weekend. Furthermore, this is the location where the abdominal surgeon scheduled to see Mary just 3 days from now on Monday, Oct. 2 operates in. This way, she'll be in place whether she needs emergency surgery over the weekend or the abdominal surgeon deems surgery as an option on Monday.

CHAPTER SIX
LIFE AT THE CANCER CENTER

Wow! Things are really starting to happen so fast! Mary's being transported by ambulance to Sarah Cannon while I'm driving to our home to pick up some personal belongings for the both of us. Once at home, I first called our daughter plus some other family and friends to update them on Mary being admitted to Sarah Cannon. I asked all of them to be in prayer for Mary and the staff at Sarah Cannon. I then retrieved our personal items and while driving to Sarah Cannon, it dawned on me that the Oncologist never went over any of the results from Mary's biopsy and PET scan. I just shrugged it off and thanked God that Mary was comfortable again and headed to a place to receive proper care and treatment.

Upon arriving at Sarah Cannon, I was met and directed to Mary's room by the attending surgeon with whom her Oncologist had spoken earlier. He was all business and rightfully so. He said that Mary would be under close observation and that she would be both properly medicated and hydrated through IV. He wanted her to abstain from eating any soft or solid foods in case emergency surgery would be necessary. However, he would allow her to chew ice and eat an occasional popsicle. This pleased Mary since she loved to chew ice!

When awakening Saturday morning, we both smiled at each other and commented on what a much-needed pleasant night's rest we had. Mary's color had returned to her face and she actually had an appetite to eat something. I reminded her that the surgeon had restricted her from any kind of soft or solid foods and that she could just eat ice chips/popsicles. Her stomach was really growling so I called for a nurse to see if there was any way that maybe Mary could be reassessed and could eat some soft or possibly solid food. Since Mary's condition had improved and stabilized overnight, he felt comfortable to allow her to drink some Ensure and observe how she handled that. She passed with flying colors!

We had a nice visit when our daughter stopped by to spend some time with us. She had her hands full with a 6 ½ month old daughter but was able to get away for a bit with her husband being home on the weekend. She was somewhat excited about attending the annual family reunion on my mom's side of the family the next day. She was excited because it would be the first time for extended family to meet her daughter but very disappointed, as were we, that her mom and I would be unable to attend. We told her that her mom's condition had improved, stabilizing since the previous night and that basically we were waiting to meet with the abdominal surgeon on Monday. Before our daughter left, we prayed for Mary's healing, guidance and wisdom for the medical staff and for her safe return home.

The rest of the day was mostly pleasant and we found ourselves mainly engaged in normal conversation between a husband and wife. We talked about how blessed we were to have two wonderful children who each had a child of their own along with each one having spouses that were tailored made for them. How we had earlier in the year celebrated 35 years of marriage and how both of us had been retired since the previous December. Then fortunately or unfortunately, I guess depending on your perspective, the conversation turned as serious as serious can be. Mary said that I should consider entertaining what my life would be like without her. I honestly didn't want to hear it much less discuss it!

She started by saying I know you don't want to talk about; it nobody would. However, you and I both have shared about no matter how much we pray, stand on God's promises and walk by faith both our spirits remain troubled. I just think that it would be wise to make sure you have things in order in case I don't make it. She further stated that once procedures and treatments start, we can't take for granted that she would be in a sound enough frame of mind to have these conversations. As much as I didn't want to, I found myself not only agreeing with her but strangely having an unexpected peace and contentment deep within my spirit. In hindsight, this would be one of those moments that would assist in laying the foundation of what my future would hold. I promised Mary that from that point forward I would open up more to the Lord for guidance and direction concerning my future without her. Our prayer that night was for God's will to be done in both our lives. That His plans and purposes would prevail in our lives. That we would be totally submitted to Him, trusting and depending on Him to see us through regardless of the path He has prepared for us, in Jesus' name, Amen!

It's now Sunday, Oct. 1. Mary and I again had a very pleasant night's rest. We awoke to several phone calls enquiring as to whether we would be attending the family reunion that day. We replied to all that unfortunately we would not be attending and just continue to lift us, especially Mary up in prayer. The nurse that morning informed us that a nutritionist would be stopping by at some point today to come up with some sort of a meal plan for her. We were both excited with this news which sounded very promising. We both concluded that this meant that Mary was moving in the right direction. It's moments like these that would prompt me to question the troubling in my spirit.

That afternoon, the couple that we went to Biloxi MS with stopped by for a visit. Honestly, I can't remember if they brought Subway sandwiches or I walked to the Subway on site bringing back sandwiches for three of us excluding Mary. Regardless, when I started eating my sandwich, Mary commented that it smelled so good that she wanted a bite of it. Acknowledging her request, I handed her a 6" part of the sandwich which she promptly started eating. As she was eating, the nutritionist walked in and smilingly commented, well now, it appears that you have decided to proceed without my input for your meal plan. The expression on Mary's face was priceless! She looked like the kid that got caught with their hand in the cookie jar. We all erupted with laughter! The nutritionist encouraged Mary to continue eating the sandwich but cautioned her not to get too carried away as to allow her digestive system to slowly process solid food once more. The nutritionist then went over different meal options with Mary which concluded with the two of them agreeing on a plan and the nutritionist leaving with a smile.

Once our friends had left, it was early evening and Mary had a terrified look on her face. She wanted me to cuddle as close as I could to her in the hospital bed and just hold her. She started shivering, sobbing and told me that she was really scared about what she was facing. This woman of faith and strength who the night before was so concerned about my well-being was suddenly embraced by a spirit of fear like she had never experienced before. She repeatedly kept saying just hold me, just hold me, just hold me! The reality was beginning to set in that she would be seeing the abdominal surgeon tomorrow morning and she would be having surgery in the next day or two. I just continued to hold her, pray for her and shed tears with her. Truth is, while I tried my best to be strong for her, I was very scared and afraid myself!

It's moments like these that make me realize why my spirit was troubled! It has nothing to do with a lack of faith! It does have everything to do with choosing to draw closer to God in these moments as opposed to doubting His plan and pushing Him away! The scripture that the Holy Spirit brought to my remembrance at this moment was, "Draw near to God and He will draw near to you." (James 4:8 NASB) I shared this scripture with Mary before saying our prayers and retiring for the night.

The next morning, we were awakened by my cell phone ringing. It was a call from the receptionist at the abdominal surgeon's office to confirm Mary's appointment for that afternoon at 1:30 P.M. We were somewhat caught off guard by the call, we were both under the assumption that with Mary being hospitalized that that appointment had been cancelled and the consultation would be at the hospital. The receptionist replied by stating that she would notify the surgeon of

Mary's whereabouts and also cancel the appointment.

Wow! Within an hour, the abdominal surgeon and his assistant were front and center in Mary's room. We had heard that he had an impeccable reputation as a surgeon and that he could come across as being very arrogant considering he was the most requested abdominal surgeon in this area. Remember, he's the surgeon that the physicians we have met along the way would want operating on them. This has always been very comforting especially if surgery would be necessary.

After introducing he and his assistant, the first words out of his mouth were, "Mrs. Mary Blakely, you are a woman who a lot of people are concerned about your health and well-being of which I include myself among them. I just arrived early this morning after being out of town for a week and I find your medical file on top of a stack of files on my desk. After reading your file, I understand how and why yours is the first case that demanded my attention. I have spent the last hour familiarizing myself with all aspects of your condition. I have been in contact with one of my closest associates along with your Oncologist to devise a plan that would be best not just for your immediate health but for your long-term health as well."

He proceeded to tell us that the results of the PET scan indicated that the preliminary diagnosis of the CT scan performed on Labor Day was unfortunately very accurate. That there was a tumor of significant size that originated in the duodenum that had spread via the bile duct to the liver and to a lymph node. That the activity was concerning and appeared to be cancerous in nature. By definition based on this report, Mary had Stage 4 cancer with only a 5% chance of surviving. He further stated that of course the cancer diagnosis would have to be verified by having received proper pathology based on a biopsy of the tumor.

Due to the nature of the diagnosis, time is of the upmost importance. Because of this, the best course of action would not be for him to operate and try to remove as much of the tumor as possible but to yield to his colleague. His colleague had perfected a procedure in which he inserts a collapsed miniscule stent into the restricted area of the duodenum. Once inserted, the stent expands when pulled from either end opening up the restriction and then conforming to the wall of the duodenum. This would serve two purposes. It would open up the restricted area to allow a specimen of the tumor to be collected for pathology plus allow Mary's small intestine to once again function properly. This procedure would accomplish the goals at hand in the least evasive way possible. The recovery time from this procedure would be 2-4 weeks whereas the recovery time from abdominal surgery would be 6-8 weeks. With the potential cancer having already spread, Mary needs to recover as quickly as possible to begin radiation and chemotherapy immediately thereafter.

The surgeon told us that his colleague has already scheduled Mary for this procedure to take place at 9:00 A.M. tomorrow morning of course with our approval. Mary and I told him how much we appreciated all that he had done for her in such a short period of time and that absolutely we were both on board with this procedure being done tomorrow morning. I told him how much I appreciated his willingness to yield to his colleague for what was best for Mary. However, I confided in him that this is not turning out the way that I thought it would. In my mind, I thought he would just simply remove the tumor from Mary's body and if any cancer were present the Oncologist would treat with chemotherapy. He stated that in Mary's case, the potential cancer has advanced to the point that we're going to have to go about things differently than we normally would. He further stated that it's good that you all are praying people because we're probably going to need help from the Almighty on this one. However, try to be of good cheer because Mary could be one of the 5%. Somebody has to be! He then said his goodbyes and was on his way to his next patient.

Once the surgeon left, Mary and I immediately prayed for the procedure that she would be having tomorrow morning. We prayed for Mary, that the presence of the Lord would be upon her providing comfort and contentment resulting with her being in a peaceful frame of mind to receive healing. We continued to pray that by Jesus' stripes that she was healed whether it be supernaturally, surgically, medicinally or a combination thereof. Regardless of how the healing manifests, God receives the glory, the honor and the praise! We prayed for the GI physician who would be performing the procedure and his staff for guidance and wisdom, that the desired results of this procedure would be accomplished according to plan. We thanked God that He loves us so much that He provided a way for us. That in the name of Jesus we can enter into His very presence and petition Him with our prayers and concerns when faced with such a circumstance as this.

After praying, we both expressed how we felt that a weight had been lifted off our shoulders. About that time, a fellow knocked on the open door and asked if he could come in and pray with us for anything. He introduced himself as a pastor from a church in White House TN, he stated that as the Lord led, he would go around to different medical facilities in the Middle TN area and pray for folks. We told him that would be great and Mary proceeded to tell him about her situation. He anointed her with oil and we laid hands on her with the pastor leading in prayer. During that time of prayer, heaven came down and the three of us were praying in the Spirit, rejoicing and just praising God! He said that he had 30 minutes or so before he had to head back home and if I needed to go get coffee or a bite to eat that he could keep Mary company until I returned. I took him up on his offer and headed downstairs to get some coffee.

While I was waiting in line for coffee, I started texting family and friends that Mary wouldn't be having surgery today but instead would be having a procedure tomorrow morning. When I glanced up from texting, my son and daughter-in-law had just entered the facility and were headed my way. We embraced and they enquired as to whether Mary was still in surgery or not and I updated them about the new game plan. They had made arrangements for her parents to come up from Alabama to watch their almost 15month-old son so they could be there during and after Mary's surgery. They asked me if I ever received the results of the PET scan, I acknowledged that I had by pulling a folded copy from my back pocket. Before handing to them to read, I stated that it's not a good report. My daughter-in-law being a charge nurse at Vanderbilt, shook her head from side to side while reading the report. There was no need for words, her expression said it all.

After getting coffee we headed to Mary's room. Upon entering, I introduced my son and his wife to the Pastor who was keeping Mary company. The Pastor stood up, gave me his calling card and told me to please call if he could be of further assistance regardless of the time of day. He stated that he and his congregation would be in continued prayer for our family before excusing himself and heading on his way.

It was good to have our son and his wife there simply for their presence and conversation. This was not our daughters-in-law first rodeo concerning cancer. Her father thankfully is a colon cancer survivor. She had been there for her mother while her father was going through his battle with cancer. Even though Mary's diagnosis was more dire than our son's father-in-law's was, you hold on to any piece of information that provides hope and encouragement during this time. After spending some quality time with one another, they said their goodbyes and headed back home.

By this time, it was early evening when the GI physician's assistant came in with instructions concerning the procedure being performed tomorrow morning. Typical information on the most part, nothing to eat or drink after a certain time and Mary would be taken down around 7:00 A.M. for the 9:00 A.M. procedure. After he left, Mary and I both were comforted by the professionalism and compassion that had been expressed to us throughout the day by the entire medical staff. We shortly thereafter said our prayers and settled in for the night. It had been one heck of a day emotionally but at least we were starting to make progress concerning Mary's diagnosis and treatment.

The next morning arrived rather quickly! Medical staff woke us up around 6:00 A.M. to prep Mary for her procedure that morning. I fortunately was able to spend a few minutes with her in prayer beforehand. As soon as we finished prayer, Mary spit up a bunch of blood. This had never happened before. The medical staff immediately ushered me from the room and within 5 minutes were headed to the procedural floor with Mary. The thought crossed my mind, what if this was the last time I see her alive!

At this time, I'm a nervous wreck! I'm waiting in line for coffee and a breakfast sandwich hoping to get something in my system to calm me down. While waiting, my mind is flooded with scripture and I'm just trying to grasp one to meditate on for comfort. I start reciting over and over in my mind, God's perfect love casts out all fear! It's amazing how my spirit, mind and body received this comfort from God's word. Even though the circumstance hadn't changed, God was sustaining me by His word in the midst of the present circumstance. Thankfully, we have this resource available to us through Christ 24/7. Remember that in John 16:33 Jesus states, "In the world you will have tribulation, but take courage, I have overcome the world." I believe that in this very moment, this truth was sown in my heart and resonated in my spirit as never before! Even though this circumstance may not be resolved the way I would like for it to, my God will never leave me or forsake me!

After receiving my coffee and sandwich, I proceeded to the waiting area to see if I could get an update on Mary from the medical staff. What seemed like an eternity but had only been a couple of hours, the GI physician appeared and proceeded to bring me up to date on Mary's condition. He stated that due to Mary spitting up blood, they slotted her in earlier than scheduled. That when he proceeded with the endoscopy, that the restriction in Mary's duodenum had almost completely closed. However, he was able to install the stent which opened up the restriction as planned, he was then able to obtain a specimen of the tumor for pathology. He further stated that unfortunately, Mary's small intestine area had suffered a lot of damage and that her recovery time was going to be on the high end of about 4 weeks. The great news is that the restriction no longer exists which will alleviate a good bit of the pain that she has been experiencing. Before excusing himself, he stated that Mary would be back in her room in about an hour or so and that he would stop by before day's end to check on her progress.

After he left, I went outside and walked around the facility for a few minutes just talking to the Lord and collecting my thoughts. I thanked Him that His timing is perfect! That the procedure was accomplished both successfully and in His timing! I then called the kids updating them on their mother's condition. As I was walking back to Mary's room, I began to pray for her small intestine to heal in accordance with God's plan for her life. I was surprised by the way in which I found myself praying! At some point, I had transitioned from praying for my plan (which would be an immediate and total healing), to simply praying for what Mary's most pressing immediate need was. Once arriving at Mary's room, I laid in the recliner and dozed off until they brought her back to the room.

Fortunately, when Mary came to after being in her room for a bit, I was sitting at her side to greet her with a smile. She managed a brief smile as well and asked how the procedure had gone. I proceeded to tell her that the goals had been accomplished but her small intestine had suffered more damage than anticipated. Due to this, her healing time would be more in line with 4 weeks as opposed to 2. She asked me how I was managing all of this and I responded by saying I'm hanging in there like a loose tooth as opposed to a hair in a biscuit. This response accomplished what it was supposed to which was both of us busting out laughing. Seriously, I told her that it's really tough and that I would swap places with her if I could. She immediately reacted with I wouldn't want to swap places; I would much rather be in the bed as opposed to the one sitting beside the bed. I nodded in agreement and told her that the GI physician would be up at some point to check on her progress.

When the GI physician arrived, I walked over and greeted him at the door. He suggested that I leave for about 30 minutes so that he could have a private consultation with Mary. I guess the expression on my face gave away what I was thinking because he then said that he would explain to me the purpose of this when I returned. Taking advantage of this time I went to get something to eat and made a couple of phone calls. Upon returning to Mary's room, the physician was sitting next to Mary's bed engaged in conversation and laughing. This really did warm my heart to see my Mary feeling and behaving more like her usual self. I immediately asked if I could get in on some of this because I could sure use a laugh or two myself. The physician stated that my timing was perfect as he proceeded to go over some particulars concerning Mary's routine for the next few days prior to her being discharged. He then wished Mary his best and asked if I would join him in the hall for a few minutes.

He began to explain to me how just a couple of years ago that he was in a similar situation as Mary. How his diagnosis prompted him to brainstorm which led to him designing and inventing the stent which he had just implanted into Mary earlier today. He stated that as we speak, he is cancer free and he believed that the Lord allowed him to go through this battle to obtain the wisdom needed to invent this stent to assist in future patients healing process. Since then, whenever he had a patient with a similar diagnosis, he felt impressed to share his experience with them for encouragement. He stated that even though his diagnosis wasn't quite as serious as Mary's, that he would not have survived if the Lord had not intervened. He continued by saying that the reason he shares his experience separately with each spouse is because it removes the emotion involved in the circumstance. This allows each person to fully receive and comprehend the testimony being put forth. Before departing, he stated that the two of you have a hard road ahead of you but try to remain cheerful. Remember that Jesus' yoke is easy, His burden is light, that milkshakes, smoothies are your best friend and I hope we meet again someday under better circumstances!

I then went back into Mary's room and sit at her bedside to compare notes so to speak pertaining to our conversations with her GI physician. She started by saying that he had shared with her the similar experience that he had and how the Lord blessed him with the wisdom to design the stent. How he had such a gentle disposition that really put her at ease to receive his testimony. I stated that our conversation was pretty much identical to the one they had. I asked her how she was feeling, she said that she could tell a difference in her mid-section that it wasn't cramping any longer. That she was more relaxed and felt less pain. We then thanked God for the healing being manifested in Mary's body and said our prayers before retiring for the evening.

The next morning, we were greeted by the dietician assigned to devise a meal plan for Mary. She was the same one who had caught Mary with a 6-inch sub in her mouth just 3 days earlier. Her first words were absolutely no Subway sandwiches this time around. We all started laughing but she emphasized how serious she was about what Mary could eat. Mary and I expressed to her that we were aware that Mary's digestive system had been damaged, was in a healing phase and that she had our undivided attention. The plan implemented consisted mainly of Ensure with an occasional smoothie and/or milkshake worked in depending on how Mary's digestive system functioned. The goal was to have Mary eating pureed foods prior to her being discharged in a few days. She began sipping her first Ensure and was off and running.

The rest of the day was very pleasant and peaceful considering you're in a cancer ward at the hospital. Having said that, while I may have appeared to be calm on the outside, in my mind thoughts are racing to and fro. All the "what if's" trying to take over and gain control. The spiritual battle really is in our minds. That's why it is so important during these storms of life to cry out to Jesus for help! To be aware to cast down your imagination that goes against God's word and to renew your mind with the washing away of God's word! While I was going through this battle in my mind to regain some sort of stability both spiritually and mentally, Mary was lying in bed less than 5 feet from me pretty much just resting and sipping on an occasional Ensure, appearing not to have a care in the world. I couldn't help but wonder what was going on in her mind!

The next time that Mary was open for conversation, I asked her what was going on in her innermost thoughts. She said that even though she had some fear and apprehension of what the future might hold, she had been reviewing her life more and more each day reflecting on how blessed she had been over the course of her life. How God had brought her through the tough times in life both prior to and after her making a commitment to accept Christ as Lord and Saviour! That is what she's holding onto to give her strength and courage which motivates her to press forward despite how she feels. That she's at peace for whatever plans God has in store for her whether it be to live many more years or a much shorter period of time. She would prefer the former rather than the latter but she has accepted the reality that she's in God's hands.   I responded with there's no better place for you to be than in the hands of our God.

Actually, that's true for all of us regardless of what we're dealing with in this life! There's just more emphasis placed on your situation because we're talking about you possibly dying. Whereas you have a peace and contentment to a certain extent about dying, I'm simply not ready to let you go! I can't imagine having to live the rest of my life without you. You're my helpmate, my best friend, my travelling companion pretty much my everything in this world! Even though we've been married 35 years, we're just getting started retirement wise! You've been retired less than a year and we were planning to do a lot of travelling until this happened! I'm just having a very hard time trying to understand how and why this is happening to you of all people. Mary then began leading in prayer mainly praying for me to be comforted. We said our good night's and thankfully went right to sleep!

When you're staying overnight in a medical facility, typically you'll be awakened by staff at some point and not of your own doing. This morning would be no different as we were greeted by the abdominal surgeon and his assistant. Their visit was to report to us the pathological results of the biopsy performed on the tumor. Unfortunately, the results confirmed what had been suspected since the CT scan was performed on Labor Day. That Mary in fact had a cancerous tumor in her duodenum that had spread to her liver and to a lymph node as well. The difference being this time around that we had physical evidence of the cancer which was identified as adenocarcinoma. The abdominal surgeon stated that although this is an aggressive type of cancer it usually responds well to proper treatment. However, in this case, the cancer has metastasized and time is of the essence! The plan for now is for Mary to receive proper rest and nourishment to improve her overall physicality to start treatment in approximately 4 weeks. We'll keep you hospitalized for a couple more days to get you started on the right track before releasing you to your Oncologist. He further stated that he would forward all reports to Mary's Oncologist so he could establish and implement a proper treatment plan when she was ready. He then excused himself and his assistant to proceed to their next patient.

After they left the room, Mary and I hugged with the two of us just sobbing like never before. Our greatest fear had just become reality! I can't speak for Mary, but I was somewhat traumatized, stunned and in shock! I left the room to get a drink of water and tried to put on a good face to be strong for her but sometimes you just can't pull it off. This was one of those times. Upon returning to her room, she saw right through it! I took my place by her bedside and we pretty much just continued our conversation from the previous night. She gently took hold of my right hand and proceeded to confirm to me that she was good with everything that was happening. She said that while like you, I certainly don't understand everything, but I've had my Garden of Gethsemane moment having accepted God's will in this situation for my life. While I continue to pray for healing, I also pray for courage and strength to endure this season that the Lord has allowed me to be in. Knowing that this cancer is not from God but from the devil, the enemy always overplays his hand. We know that all things work together for good to those that love God, to those who are the called according to His purpose! She ended by saying again that she's concerned about me, that I need to prepare for life without her but keep hoping and praying for the best.

I responded to Mary with I know everything that you're telling me is true! I believe with everything that I am, that God is using you as a vessel to help prepare me for the journey ahead that He has planned for me. Having said that, while it may resonate with my spirit, my heart and mind are not there yet. While I continue to pray for your complete healing, I also pray for your daily needs to be provided as well as me allowing the Holy Spirit to minister to and help prepare me for the season I'm in as well. There's an abundance of casting down imaginations and crucifying the flesh going on throughout each day. I know in my spirit that this trial is drawing me closer to the Lord than I've ever been before. I told her that I wish that I was stronger and could be more encouraging for her, that she seemed to be the one providing the support my way. She pulled me close and whispered that as long as you're sitting in this chair next to me, you're providing all the encouragement that I need from you. You're doing just fine!

CHAPTER SEVEN
LIFE AT HOME

We've made it to Sunday October 8, 2017. After what has been the longest week of our lives, Mary was discharged to go home today. The abdominal surgeon's assistant provided the necessary paperwork and instructions to be followed upon discharge. I told him that Mary had been experiencing some abdominal pain, that I wanted to make sure that she could continue to take the pain meds that we had at home. He stated that would be fine, that she should be in pain because she has cancer. I took that to heart meaning that if Mary wasn't in pain that the cancer would be gone. This is a point of reference to remember for a future chapter. I allowed this way of thinking to set me up for a future disappointment!

Upon arriving home, Mary wanted to be seated in her favorite spot. On the loveseat in the living room next to the double pictured window. She hadn't seen sunshine in over a week! This was her quiet place in our home. The place where she spent her time with the Lord by reading her devotionals and praying for the many people on her prayer list. After getting her settled on the loveseat, I set up a tv tray where she could easily reach her Ensure and ice water. As I was walking to the rec room, I turned and glanced at her smiling, sitting in the sunshine and reading just like old times. I thanked God that we were home and hopefully had turned a corner for the better in this season of life. Unfortunately, it would be short lived!

When entering the rec room, I added more prescriptions to the already numerous prescriptions on the pool table. I cleared my mind and focused on the task at hand. As had been commonplace for the last month, I proceeded to apply post it notes in front of each row of prescriptions to ensure that each would be administered appropriately. I was really looking forward to Mary beginning her recovery this week to regain her overall physicality to begin treatment next month. Mentally, I was preparing a menu for the week ahead that had been recommended by the dietician. I was praying that Mary would have an appetite for some of the pureed foods that were recommended. She had no interest for that type of food at the hospital mainly sticking with Ensure and smoothies.

For supper that night I prepared some mashed potatoes and peas which normally would be one of our favorites. As far back as I can remember, I always hollowed out the center of my pile of mashed potatoes and added peas in the middle thus resulting in what I called a bird's nest. Mary always made fun of me for doing this but it always provided some laughter and I continue to do it to this very day. Tonight would be very different! The meal would have to be pureed for Mary to be able to consume properly hopefully with no complications. I had decided to eat pureed food as well to show support and encouragement towards my wife. It was a disaster! Drinking mashed potatoes and peas is a far cry from eating traditionally with a fork. Mary immediately got sick and started vomiting which prompted me to do the same. Fortunately, we were well prepared for any vomiting with strategically located trash cans with liners placed throughout our home.

Unfortunately, this aggravated Mary's abdominal area causing the pain to intensify. After we both had somewhat recovered from this episode, I helped her get prepared for hopefully what would be a good night's rest in our own bed. I first administered the newly prescribed medication which would assist in healing Mary's duodenum which had been damaged by the tumor. This medication thankfully settled her stomach to the point where she was able to take her pain meds and keep them down. I always pray over and ask God to bless and anoint any medication that I provide to someone or take myself, just like I do my food before I eat. A dear friend of mine that I have known since we were four years old encouraged me to do this years ago. Made sense to me so I've been doing it for years. Mary and I said our prayers, thanked the Lord for being in our own bed and thankfully fell immediately to sleep.

When awaking the next morning, Mary was still sleeping peacefully. I continued to lay in bed for a few minutes before I finally got up and immediately headed to the kitchen to make some coffee. I call it my Jesus and java time in the morning. When I was working I had to fit this time in whenever I could because of working so many different hours. Since I retired, the Lord impressed upon me to be still and know that He is God by dedicating time first thing each morning to Him as to receive my marching orders from Him to carry out my assignments for that day. As I spent time with Him that morning, He impressed upon me to go to Smoothie King and have them specially prepare two large smoothies for Mary. The physician who implanted the stent in Mary's duodenum had given me a list of ingredients to have added to Mary's smoothies which would assist in her healing. Smoothie King graciously obliged my request as I found myself heading back home feeling very encouraged about the day to come.

Once arriving back home, as soon as I walked in the house, I could hear Mary throwing up. I immediately ran to our bedroom in the back of our home to comfort her. In the 30 minutes that I had been gone she went from resting peacefully to being very nauseous. I just sit on the bed, held her in my arms and prayed in the Spirit for several minutes. She had somewhat settled down when I told her that I had a specially made smoothie for her to sip on throughout the day. She said that sounded good and wanted to give it a try. She took a couple of sips and immediately started vomiting again. What seemed like a promising idea had once again resulted in a disaster. I got her cleaned up and she said all she wanted to do was to go to sleep. So, we held hands and prayed until she fell back to sleep.

I then went outside and I immediately started questioning the Lord. I don't understand Lord, I went and purchased the smoothies just as you impressed upon me to do. However, the smoothie made Mary nauseous and now she doesn't want them near her. Help me understand Lord! The Lord impressed upon me that Mickey, it's not as much about the end result of what I have you do as it is about you being obedient in what I tell you to do. Remember, you are to walk by faith and not by sight. You're never going to fully see or realize what I accomplish when I command you to do something. It's always going to be a small piece of the finished puzzle in my timing. But your obedience by doing what I command you to do will always bring blessings into your life! I know this is hard for you as it is for most of my children but you need to stop trying to figure it out! Just trust me! As you trust Me, you'll be able to rest and have peace in Me! I replied with Lord I will try!!!

Unfortunately, concerning Mary, the rest of this week would be the same as today. She would continue to be nauseous, eat and drink very little mainly just sleeping. I didn't know what to do, I felt helpless! I cried out to the Lord for guidance and wisdom. He impressed upon me to call the oncology nurses hotline. So, I did! I informed them about what was happening with Mary and they immediately instructed me to bring her in to their facility. Once arriving, based upon Mary's condition, they rolled her to the treatment area reuniting her with her new best friend (head nurse) which she had met on the previous visit. That visit seemed like an eternity ago but in reality, had only been 11 days. While Mary was being treated with IV fluids and meds, I was in consultation with the oncologist going over her treatment plan.

The oncologist proceeded to inform me that he had consulted a radiologist who wanted to hit the tumor hard with 5 straight days of intense radiation. These treatments would commence on October 30th and end on November 3rd. The two of them believed that this treatment would keep the tumor somewhat in check until they could start chemotherapy on November 7th. So, Mary had 3 weeks to prepare for a full week of radiation treatments before starting chemotherapy the following week. The oncologist asked if I had any concerns about what we had discussed. I told him that based on what I have heard that the plan makes sense to me and does provide some comfort as to what to expect. I informed him that since Mary's birthday is November 7th could chemotherapy possibly start on November 8th. He looked at his calendar and stated that November 8th would work out just fine.

After the consultation, we both headed towards the treatment area to bring Mary into the loop. When we saw Mary, she looked like a totally different person. She had color in her face and was cutting up with laughter as she engaged in conversation with her new best friend. The oncologist proceeded to bring Mary up to speed on her treatment plan. She responded with a big smile almost shouting let's do it! It's amazing to see the healing effect that medication has on the human body when properly administered. Before heading back home, I expressed my concern about Mary's inability to stomach any drinks or medications when at home. The oncologist stated that today they had administered enough medications to last for a couple of days. So, just plan on coming back at 1:00 P.M. on both Wednesday and Friday for the same type of treatment. Hold off taking any more medications orally this week as to give your digestive system a break to promote healing. However, sip as much water and Ensure as you can tolerate.

When arriving back home, our daughter called and said that she was bringing over some healthy soups, high protein milk and other essentials that would help with her mom's healing as time permitted. Mary also received a call from her sister in Indiana who wanted to come down and help out with things. Mary's sister said that she had a few loose ends to tie up by weeks end and that she would be down on Saturday October 14th. Mary and her sister are really close both relationally and in age with her sister just being 1 year older. Mary and I both were looking forward to her sister coming down for several reasons. Her being here would provide additional help for Mary's needs including fellowship and free me up to do some things that I had put on hold.

The rest of the week Mary pretty much rested in bed. When she would attempt to drink any Ensure or water, she immediately became nauseous. Of course, this was very concerning! We both were hoping that she would be able to at least consume some liquid protein to help regain her physicality. I took her to the oncologist's office on both Wednesday and Friday to receive fluids and meds from her still new best friend. This was such a blessing to help us make it to week's end. While Mary was receiving treatment during Friday's visit, her new best friend pulled me to the side and suggested that I set up an appointment with the grief therapist on site. Honestly, this caught me off guard. Even though Mary's diagnosis was dire with a 95% chance of dying, I always looked at death as a part of life and you just manned up and kept on going. I never even considered going to any kind of grief counseling. However, that still, small voice inside of me wouldn't quiet down until I made an appointment for October 26th.

The biggest change in our daily routine at home was that I moved having devotional from the living room to our bedroom closet. Except for the first day home from the hospital, Mary has been unable to read due to nauseousness, headaches and light sensitivity. I attempted to read from her bedside but the light that I required to see was too bright for her. So, I migrated into the closet which provided enough light to read our devotionals. This was a very telling sign of Mary's condition. She loved to read! Another sign was that she was having a hard time remembering scripture verses that she often quoted. She would occasionally ask me, "how does that particular scripture go?" She smilingly stated that as long as I can speak the name of Jesus, I'll be okay! Sometimes, I would just sit in the closet with the door completely closed to recite and pray scripture over her as to not disturb her sleep. One such time when I opened the closet door, Mary was sitting up on the bedside and asked me if I was okay. I responded with, no I'm not!

I'm concerned because you're not drinking anything other than some water occasionally. You've got to start receiving some nourishment into your body at some point or else you're not going to be around much longer. She didn't want to hear that saying that I didn't understand. I agreed with her saying that I didn't! About that time the doorbell rang, Mary's sister had arrived.

Mary's sister could not have arrived at a more opportune time. I immediately caught her up on what had just transpired between Mary and me. She suggested that after I got her belongings in her room, it would be a good idea for me to go visit my parents for a few hours. That would not only give me a break but also allow her to spend some time with her sister. After getting her settled, I kissed Mary goodbye and headed to my parents' home. It was about an hour's drive on a mostly secluded section of interstate. Typically, a very peaceful and somewhat scenic drive. However, on this day about halfway there, the devil started accusing me if I really loved Mary how could I upset her like I did about not eating properly. That's the last thing she needed you to do. You should have been more compassionate and understanding. I started sobbing and asking God for forgiveness in Jesus' name, asking Him to give me patience plus the Godly attributes that I would need to be the husband that Mary would require during this season. I told God that if I didn't care, I wouldn't have said anything. God responded with, Mickey, you're doing just fine. That old devil just overplayed his hand again. He thought he could discourage and push you further away from me, when in reality all he did was draw you closer to me which prompts me to draw closer to you. Isn't it comforting to have such an awesome Heavenly Father to depend on during our times of distress!

Once arriving at my parents, I became very emotional even before I dismounted from my vehicle. It had been approximately 6 weeks since I had last seen my parents. We had occasionally spoke on the phone concerning what was transpiring with Mary. The conversations usually ended with me breaking down emotionally and sobbing to my momma. When my daddy answered the phone, he would reply son I don't know what to say or do and hand the phone to my momma. I'm the oldest of 5 children and have always been and always will be a momma's boy. Now I find myself walking towards their door just an emotional, sobbing hot mess!

When my momma greeted me at the door my emotions and sobbing peaked out reaching a new level. We hugged each other like we had done twice before when her/my granddaughter/niece and daughter/sister had died. She comforted me by reminding me that even though we still experience moments of emptiness and discomfort due to their deaths that God has and will continue to sustain and comfort us. She continued by saying I can only imagine how hard this is for you, you just continue to lean on the Lord son and he will keep you in perfect peace in spite of the circumstance (Isaiah 26:3 KJV). I know that you're aware of this but sometimes in the midst of our despair we need someone to gently remind us of God's promises. Even though we have occasional disagreements, once again my momma comforts me as only a mother can when it matters most.

Once inside, our conversation pretty much consisted of me answering any questions concerning Mary and if there was anything that they could do to provide any assistance. I told them that Mary's sister had just travelled down today to stay as long as needed which is why I was able to visit today. Ya'll just keep praying, touching base by phone and I'll visit whenever time permits. Besides, I'd already received what I came for before I even entered yall's home! We all busted out with laughter as we hugged and said our goodbyes. It was a short but much needed visit for all of us. As I drove back home, I found myself thanking God that my parents were still alive and in good health to provide support for me during this season of my life. Thank you, Jesus!!!

Arriving back home, it was comforting having Mary's sister there to provide support. She pretty much kept to herself, as did I most of the time. She had no issue bringing to my attention that she was there to help but I wasn't allowing her to do so. I told her that I was open to any suggestions that would benefit the care that Mary requires. Up to this point when something needed to be done, I'm in the habit of just doing it. From that point forward we worked in a manner that was beneficial for the three of us. I know that Mary greatly benefited by the precense of her sister. She told me that it was awesome to be able to spend time with her on a daily basis.

The following night was October 15th, 2017. It was exactly 1 week to the hour that Mary had been home from the hospital and unfortunately experienced the pureed food debacle. This time, instead of being a food related abdominal episode, Mary was passing blood from her rectum. We had just gotten her cleaned up and put on her pajamas when she needed to use the toilet. We considered this a big victory at first! Her having to use the toilet was an indication that she had processed enough substance to produce a bowel movement. However, when she stood up from the toilet unfortunately, she was passing blood.

I called ahead to the ER at Centennial Medical Center to alert them that I was bringing in an established cancer patient. They then notified Sarah Cannon Cancer Center, which shares the same campus, to have a room ready to receive Mary upon arrival. This is such a blessing because this protocol allows cancer patients to circumvent being possibly exposed to various germs from incoming patients at the ER. The medical staff as always were very accommodating and immediately escorted Mary to her assigned room. After further examination, the attending physician contacted the GI physician's office which concluded that they would conduct an endoscopy first thing Monday morning.

Once Mary was settled in for the night, her sister and I located the nearest Mickey D's (McDonald's) purchasing coffee and apple pies before heading back to a sitting area at the medical facility. We were both still pretty hyped up by the string of events that had led up to this moment. Her first comment to me was geez, what a way to end a day. I responded with even though the last couple of hours has been a whirlwind, I find comfort in the fact that Mary is being tended to by medical professionals which honestly gives me a break both mentally and physically. I would much rather be at home with Mary resting comfortably however, I've learned to take advantage of these situations when they occur. Typically, I'm continuously at her side to comfort and spend as much time with her as possible without disturbing her rest. She responded with I can't believe this is happening to my baby sister!

This is a living nightmare! It's one thing to be updated over the phone with Mary's diagnosis but to be here in person and now experience what you guys' life has been like over the past 6 weeks is somewhat overwhelming! While my mind was racing forward concerning contacting the kids, I told her that you just try to stay in the moment and talk to the Lord. We ended with that and headed back to Mary's room to settle in for the night.

The GI physician who would be performing the endoscopy on Mary graced our presence bright and early the following morning. He informed us that the goal was to examine the area where the stent had been inserted into Mary's duodenum and to cauterize any areas that were actively bleeding. He stated that this should be a rather routine procedure that would last approximately one hour from start to finish. Once the GI physician left, Mary, her sister and I prayed for guidance and direction for him and his team. That whatever was causing the bleeding would be evident and easily corrected. We prayed for peace and comfort over Mary's spirit, mind and body as to receive the healing that is and would be manifesting in her body. We asked these things in the name of our Lord and Savior, Jesus Christ!

Once the procedure was finished, the GI physician pulled me to the side for a private consultation. The news that he had to convey was troubling to say the least. He stated that quite honestly, Mary's duodenum has suffered a significant amount of damage. Even though the stent has opened and conformed perfectly to the duodenum's walls, the area is a bloody mess! There were several areas that I was able to cauterize successfully however, there are still some areas that I was unable to stop from further bleeding. The bleeding at this point has been somewhat minimized, which is good, but from this point forward there will continue to be some blood loss showing up in Mary's stools. We'll keep her in residence for the remainder of the week for observation and to administer IV fluids and meds to help promote healing to her duodenum. I thanked him for what he was able to accomplish, he wished me good luck upon departing.

I shared the information I had received with Mary's sister and then we each made phone calls to both family and friends with the updated information. We then proceeded back to Mary's room to wait her return from the procedure. While waiting, my mind was wandering all over the place, mainly concerning what Mary's mindset, countenance and appetite would be. Of course, I was hoping that she would be feeling well, well enough to want something to eat or drink by day's end. The GI physician had told me earlier to be patient with her concerning her food intake, that if she could tolerate a few sips of Ensure by day's end, that would be a huge success.

When returning to the room. Mary had recovered very well from the anesthesia and was cutting up laughing with the medical staff. This was such a blessing to see! She immediately requested something to drink that her mouth and throat were very dry. Her nurse honored the request by providing water, ice chips and Ensure. She instructed Mary to take it slow as to give her system a chance to adapt to receiving liquids at this point. She suggested that maybe she should just eat some ice chips and progress from there. Mary loved this idea because she enjoyed chewing soft ice.

Once the nurse left, I returned to my usual position which was at Mary's bedside. We held hands, gently kissed one another and thanked God that she was feeling as well as she did. She just grinned, shook her head and commented on what a roller coaster ride this had been for the last almost couple of months. I replied with, I know, it's hard to get somewhat settled or relaxed, as soon as you do it seem's that something happens to rock the boat. I'm just thankful that you're feeling better right now and we're able to enjoy each other's company. She asked me what time I needed to leave to go to the Titans game that night and I responded with I had totally forgot about it! Mary and her sister both encouraged me to go to the game and try to enjoy myself. So, I did somewhat reluctantly!

Heading to the game I had a multitude of thoughts racing through my mind. I would be meeting my son at the seats that we had occupied watching Titans games for the last 17 years. While that brought me some comfort, tonight's game was being aired nationwide for Monday Night Football on ESPN. So, my first task was to find a parking place which was proving to be harder than usual because downtown Nashville was a zoo! After parking, I had plenty of time to think about things since I had to park further away than I normally would. While walking towards Nissan Stadium, I was thinking about how to respond to people when asked about how Mary was doing and how am I holding up. At this point, I knew that numerous people would be in attendance who I had met throughout my life and were aware of what was going on with Mary. The Holy Spirit comforted me by impressing upon me to be who I am in Jesus within each relationship that I encountered that night.

Once arriving at my seat, I embraced my son for a few moments and almost immediately thereafter it was a fairly consistent flow of encounters amongst family, friends, church and work acquaintances. One thing that I've learned on this journey is people's intentions are to encourage, comfort and support you whether their words or actions reflect this or not. It really is a tough spot to be in! I'm as guilty as anyone who has said or done something stupid in attempting to provide these things for someone during a challenging time in life. Truth is, most of these folks were experiencing some sort of challenge because they also had an acquaintanceship with Mary. Keeping this in mind, I acknowledged and embraced every person that night regardless of actions, inactions or words spoken between us. We all needed it! It was no time for dissecting what "God's got this" means! Chances are it means something different for each person represented that night.

When leaving the game, I checked my text messages and had received one from a dear friend of mine. He grew up in West Nashville as did I and we worked together at the Post Office as well. He just wanted me to know that Mary was in his thoughts and prayers. That if we needed anything to let him know. Despite differences in our faith, we have always had each other's back throughout the years. Receiving this message of support and reassurance means the world to me. What a fitting way to end a night! Praise God! Oh, by the way, the Titans beat the Colts that night ending an 11-game losing streak against them. Almost forgot there was a football game being played that night!

It's now Saturday morning October 21, 2017. Mary finished up her stay at the hospital and came home yesterday. The last handful of days were very similar with Mary slightly progressing for the better each day. By weeks end, she was able to stomach both medications and liquids orally. This was a huge step in the right direction. We were very thankful for the outpouring of prayers and support during this stay from numerous people aware of Mary's condition. Today would be a big test! Mary, her sister and I would be driving to Kentucky not only to visit their mother but for Mary to get her hair done as well. Our kids had purchased time with a professional photographer that my son and his wife use. She would be taking family pictures of us tomorrow on Sunday afternoon.

The drive up to Kentucky was kind of touch and go. Before this illness, Mary has at times gotten carsick somewhat easily. This, combined with her current condition, presented us with a balancing act of a situation. While Mary's sister and I would be praying, Mary would sip a little, sleep a little and talk a little in cycles until we reached our first destination at the beauty parlor. Upon entering, the atmosphere within became very emotional! Mary and her sister had known the sisters that operate the business for decades and I had known them for a few years. It was very aware due to Mary's appearance that she wasn't her typical self. Normally, she would be glowing and very talkative but the underlying pain prevented this and had caught the sisters off guard.

After the embracing and tears had subsided, they got down to business and proceeded to fix Mary's hair. Word had gotten out that Mary was in town and a few of her classmates from high school stopped by to spend a little time with her. It would be the last time that Mary would be capable of paying a visit!

Now we're headed to spend some time with their mother. It's about a 20-30 minute drive along a winding up and down road to the assisted living facility where their mother resides. Surprisingly, Mary is doing quite well concerning any carsick issues at this point. It seems that with getting her hair done and spending time with some long-term friends has given her a much-needed boost! Let's also not forget the power of prayer! God has a tendency to provide what is needed in the moment! This is who God is! He can't help Himself! He is Jehovah-Jireh, God our provider! His timing is always perfect!

Our former pastor would always say," God is never late, but He's seldom ever early either!" This is a truth that I'm oftentimes trying to get through this thick skull of mine! God help us to remember that You are an ever-present help in times of trouble! Help us to yield to this truth and rest in it!

Once arriving at our second destination for the day, I could sense a lot of apprehension amongst the three of us. It ramped up even more when Mary gently but emphatically reminded us that she did not want her mother to know what was going on with her! While I didn't fully understand, I assured Mary that it was her call and I would fully support her decision. Her sister acknowledged that Mary had her support as well. Now that we were in agreement, we prayed for God's guidance and peace before heading inside. This lessened the apprehension somewhat as we entered their mother's room to visit.

Their mother is in her early 90's, hard of hearing (chooses not to wear hearing aids) and struggles with dementia. Her long-term memory is amazing at times but her shortterm memory only lasts a few minutes. She is used to being in control and typically greets anyone visiting with, "well, it's about time you decided to come visit me!" Most people laugh it off because she simply doesn't remember. She can/could be a handful at times but does have a great underlying sense of humor and you can't help but love her. At least I chose to! When entering her room, we were greeted with, you guessed it, "well, it's about time you decided to come visit me." It was perfect! We all busted out laughing because in this case she was absolutely right! It had been almost 2 months since our last visit.

The four of us relocated from their mother's room to a more spacious lounging area in the facility. Mary snuggled up to her mother on a sofa while her sister and I sat in individual chairs across from them. It was evident that Mary was struggling with her emotions as she laid her head on her mother's shoulder. While Mary was fighting back tears as best as she could, her mother had a very stern look of concern on her face. I believe in that moment that Mary was struggling with whether to tell her mother what was going on or continue to withhold this information from her. I just prayed silently in the Spirit while mouthing to Mary that it's okay whether you do or you don't. She managed to display a gentle smile my way while mouthing back thank you! Normally we would take Mary's mother for a ride around the old stomping grounds but fortunately in this case it was time for her to eat lunch in the dining area. We all said our goodbyes and Mary hugged her mother like she never had before in her life. There was an incredibly good reason for this! It would be the last time that they would ever see one another and I believe that somehow some way they were both aware of this!

The drive back home was very emotional as could be expected which honestly is a good thing. It's a medical fact that suppressing your emotions can and does affect your body and mind in detrimental ways. The three of us chose to allow our emotions to flow out in tears of sadness which at some point changed over to tears of joy and laughter. We started reminiscing about the many times that we had driven this route with their mother's commentary along the way. Like I stated earlier, their mother's long-term memory was amazing most of the time. So, as we would pass by a familiar landmark someone would shout out "if mom was here this is what she would be saying in this moment." It's amazing how time passes by so quickly when you're enjoying yourself! Before we knew it, I had pulled in the driveway and helped Mary inside to get ready for bed. It had been a very long and emotional day for her! We were very thankful that she was able to take her medication with no issues that night. We thanked the Lord for sustaining Mary throughout the day, prayed for a good night's rest and that He would continue to strengthen her for tomorrow. We were getting our family portraits taken that day at about 5 P.M.

Upon awaking from a great night's rest this Sunday morning, I could already smell coffee brewing that obviously Mary's sister had started. She was more of an early riser than Mary and I were, especially since Mary's diagnosis. With it being Sunday, it was church day. We had been attending Bedside Baptist (a close friend of ours name for home church) for the past 2 months. We really missed the congregational praise and worship along with the fellowship, but scripture tells us that wherever there are two or three gathered together in His name, that He is in the midst of them! (Matthew 18:20 KJV) With Mary's immune system being compromised, we agreed that it would be wise to attend Bedside Baptist until she was capable of being around numerous people. Some people viewed this as a lack of faith influenced by a spirit of fear while others agreed that we were exercising faith and wisdom. My two cents on this is that you need to decide based on what God is impressing upon your heart to do. Then be supportive any way that you can for the people involved. God is a holy and sovereign God who works in mysterious ways and oftentimes operates differently concerning his children!

After church, we began to get properly dressed for our photo shoot later that day. I could tell that Mary wasn't feeling as well as the previous day. I suggested that she had plenty of time to get ready and she should just lay down for an hour or so. She gave me a look that I had received a few times over the years which meant that she had this and I could leave now. While leaving the bedroom, I smilingly shook my head and blew her a kiss which in this case prompted her to manage a slight grin along with a wink prior to me closing the door. I proceeded to go outside to our covered deck to spend a little time with my sister-in-law to get her thoughts on what she'd witnessed since arriving.

I knew that Mary and her sister had plenty of opportunities to discuss what was going on with Mary. So, I straight up asked my sister-in-law if there were any concerns that I needed to be aware of. She told me that based on her conversations with Mary, that she didn't believe that Mary wanted to go through chemotherapy if it became necessary. I thought, wow! This is the first that I'm hearing of this! She said that Mary didn't come out and say it per se but my sister-in-law felt that Mary was going along with what I thought was best concerning her treatment. You could have knocked me over with a feather! Had I gotten so caught up in my emotions that I had forgotten to consider what Mary really wanted to do and just assumed that she was good with the oncologist's plan? I began to pray for guidance and wisdom as to when to talk with Mary concerning this issue. As for now, I needed to check on her and drive to the photo shoot.

When I entered our bedroom to check on Mary, not only was she ready to go but she had a radiance about her and was as beautiful as I've ever seen her. I couldn't help but think "wow" out loud! She asked me how she looked, I responded with "you look as beautiful as I've ever seen you." She replied with "thank you." While driving to our destination, which was about 20 minutes away, she let me know that she felt zapped and had very little strength. She held my hand and said I need you to literally be my rock today. I'll need you to support me when we're standing or doing any walking to the various locations for pictures. I told her that I've got you and Jesus has us. We continued to chitchat until we pulled into the parking area alongside our children's vehicles.

There was a total of 8 of us getting pictures taken that day. Mary and I, our son and his wife and their son, and finally our daughter and her husband and their daughter. So, there would be total group pictures taken along with pictures of the individual families and pictures of Mary and I with our 2 grandchildren. It was a beautiful, sunny fall day just perfect for taking pictures outside. As awesome of a day as this turned out to be, the thing I remember most is that at some point Mary was unable physically to stand and hold one of our grandkids while pictures were being taken. Instead, we had to rearrange the set with Mary sitting in a chair holding a grandchild to accommodate her condition. With the help of God's grace, we were able to finish shooting at all the different locations along with the different poses within the time that had been allotted to us.

After shooting ended, we had planned beforehand for the entire family to meet at one of our favorite restaurants to eat. We were all excited about this because with everyone's schedule's being what they were, this didn't happen very often. However, when Mary and I arrived, she told me that she was getting nauseous and there was no way that she could go inside at this point. I told her that was fine and I went inside to tell the kids that we would be going home instead. Mary kept telling me that she was so sorry, that she was messing things up concerning family time. I told her, don't be ridiculous, you don't have anything to be sorry for! This is out of your control and we'll continue to do what's best for her during this season. We kissed, told each other I love you and headed home.

Once arriving home, I backed into the garage so Mary's side would be closest to the staircase. Due to being in a flood plain, we had 12 steps to encounter before entering our home. When Mary's mother had lived with us for a couple of years, we had a chairlift installed on this particular staircase to accommodate her. Thank you Jesus that we did! Because it sure was coming in handy accommodating Mary in and out of our home. Once getting inside and after assisting her back to our bedroom, I proceeded to the kitchen to get her something cold to drink to wash her medication down. After we had gotten her ready for bed, I told her that I needed to discuss something with her if she felt up to it. She said that would be just fine!

I told her that after she had excused me from our bedroom earlier that day (which warranted me receiving that same look again), that her sister and I had talked about some things and one in particular that was concerning to me. I told Mary that her sister had implied that you didn't want to be treated with chemotherapy if it came to that. That she felt like that you were just going along with whatever

I thought was best. Mary vehemently denied even considering or alluding to not wanting to be treated with chemotherapy if that were to come into play. She further stated that I listened with great intent when my oncologist was going over what my treatment plan would be once I heal from the stent being implanted. You know me, Mickey! If I had an issue with it, you know that I would have spoken my concerns at that point. I told her that's what I thought but I just wanted to make sure based on her sister's concern. Mary further stated that "I want to live, I don't want to die! I'll consider any kind of treatment that will give me the opportunity to live for hopefully many more years to come." I comforted her by saying that you know that your sister has your best interest at heart. She is struggling like the rest of us are coping with your condition. Mary grinned, said it's been a long day and I'm going to sleep.

After surviving the busiest weekend that we had experienced since Mary's diagnosis, we were scheduled for 1 P.M. on Monday, Wednesday and Friday this week for Mary to continue to receive IV fluids and medications. Mary would be starting a daily round of radiation treatments the following week, so it was very important that she stay hydrated and hopefully ingest more protein to improve her overall physicality prior to the beginning of treatment. Also, we had an appointment with the radiologist at 3 P.M. this afternoon for Mary to get tattooed (properly marked up) before the treatments would begin the following week. We were thankful that we were able to schedule both appointments today back-to-back, also it was very convenient that the location of the two offices were in side-by-side buildings. Before leaving home, we prayed for continued strength on Mary's behalf plus guidance and wisdom for both us and the radiologist.

What a blessing it was to have Mary's sister to help assist, especially when Mary had appointments. I know that Mary appreciated it because she no longer had to wait in the wheelchair in the lobby by herself until I could find a parking space and return to take her to the oncologists' office. Occasionally they would already be checked in and sometimes Mary would be receiving treatment prior to me returning as was the case today. She looked forward to being treated by and spending time with her new best friend (charge nurse). It had been almost 2 weeks since her last visit here due to her being hospitalized the previous week. So, today was kind of a mini reunion if you will.

I can't say enough kind things about the medical community especially concerning the professionals' involved with the treatment of cancer. For the human body to properly receive treatment and for healing to manifest, there needs to be a surrounding environment of peace and comfort which causes the body to relax and receive. I want to applaud the facilities and their staffs that were involved during Mary's journey for not only the way in which they administered treatment, but as importantly the environment in which they created for her to receive treatment. Once I was exposed to the cancer medical community, they have continuously been in my thoughts and prayers even as I write. The men and women who choose to be employed in this field must have a special gifting to function in this environment day in and day out. God Bless them all!

Once Mary had finished with treatment, we proceeded to the building next door to the radiologists' office. This again would be a new experience! This first appointment would be the longest at this particular office due to Mary getting tattooed as to begin treatments next week. These radiation treatments were not part of the original plan.

However, since the tumor couldn't be surgically removed due to time restraints, Mary's oncologist consulted with this radiologist to see if radiation treatments would be a viable option. After hearing the treatment plan at a previous consult, we all decided that this would be the best option available for Mary at this time. Mary and I never blindly proceeded with any type of treatment that she was to receive on this journey. We continuously prayed for guidance and wisdom! For God to open doors and to close doors as to lead us in the steps that He has prepared for the two of us! I praise Him and I thank Him, that this is an option available to us in Jesus' name, amen!

Even though the building was next door, it still warranted driving. After dropping Mary and her sister off and finding a parking place, I had a fairly distant walk to the radiologist's facility. I was thankful that it was a nice sunny day however, I found myself becoming more anxious after each step brought me closer to the entrance of the facility. I didn't know what to perceive of this emotional distress that I was experiencing until I found myself seated inside next to Mary and her sister. As I scanned the room my heart broke! Apparently, I was being somewhat prepared for the environment in which I would soon find myself in. There was one lady in particular who pulled my heartstrings. She was obviously being treated for some type of throat/esophageal cancer as indicated by the discoloration of her throat. She was very frail in appearance but somehow someway she managed an occasional smile despite the circumstance. In this regard she reminded me of Mary.

I very quickly realized that I was surrounded by people who were fighting the same fight as Mary and I. Aware of this kindred spirit that we now share, the anxiety I was experiencing had surprisingly been replaced with a spirit of peace that passed all understanding. God works in mysterious ways! Today, He ministered to me through a lady who was literally fighting for her life! I've often wondered about whatever happened with this lady. Did she survive this terrible disease or is she rejoicing in her heavenly home. I guess either way she's celebrating. All I know is that I'm thankful that she smiled my way that day because while she was fighting for her own life, she also was helping to save mine!

While I was experiencing all of this in my mind, they had wheeled Mary back to be tattooed at some point and were now calling me back for the final consultation prior to treatment beginning. Upon entering the room, I was greeted by a nurse and Mary grinning from ear to ear wanting to know if I wanted to see her tattoos. I said, sure! After the tattoo reveal, the radiologist introduced himself; then proceeded to go over the treatment plan, asked if we had any questions and finally had us sign the necessary paperwork. He was admittedly taken aback by Mary's appearance. I thought he was somewhat joking to make Mary feel better, but he just couldn't believe that she would be 63 in a couple of weeks. I must admit that I always thought she looked 10 years younger than she was just as he did. Before leaving and after prying the radiologists' eyes off my wife, the nurse loaded us up with a nice supply of Ensure to be consumed during treatment week. Thank you, Jesus!

One area I feel that I failed miserably in during this journey as a husband was, I allowed a spirit of fear to influence my actions towards Mary for her lack of eating or drinking. I really struggled with that! I didn't understand why she wouldn't at least try to eat or drink at times to strengthen her for future treatments. This seemed to be a continual point of contention that usually ended by me leaving our bedroom in frustration! Then, I would feel guilty and within minutes return to apologize and comfort her. She would just respond by saying, "you just don't understand what I'm dealing with! I wish I knew how to make you understand but I do not! I know you're frustrated but please just continue to pray for me, comfort me and be patient with me." I promised her that I would.

Today, I find myself not taking Mary to any appointments but going to an appointment for me. I have an appointment with the grief counselor at the oncologists' office. Honestly, I never believed in this sort of thing. I've always assumed that you just ask God to help sustain you to deal with whatever comes your way in life. As I reluctantly entered the counselors' office, I was greeted by a lady with both a gentle smile and a very pleasant disposition. This immediately relieved me of any apprehension or predetermined thoughts that I had formulated on my drive here. Suddenly, instead of dreading this appointment, I found myself anticipating and somewhat intrigued about what I might learn during this session.

She informed me immediately that she was well aware of Mary's condition. That she works hand in hand with the patients who are receiving treatment through the oncologists' office along with any of their family members. She began by asking me if I had any questions or concerns about Mary's diagnosis, treatment or possible issues at home. I responded by stating that I was very concerned about Mary's lack of appetite. That while I understand that part of her digestive system is in a healing process, she appears to not be making any effort towards making progress to drink or eat anything that I provide for her. It seems that the harder I try, the more she seems to resist consuming anything put in front of her. Because of this, more times than not, I usually end up walking away in frustration! She responded with, if I may, allow me to paint a picture of what Mary's world is like which will lead me into addressing your concerns. I said, okay!

She began by stating details about Mary's diagnosis and current condition. How she has only been given a 5% chance of surviving. As soon as I heard that first comment, I lost it! I broke down and started crying like I never had before since this journey started. She provided me with some Kleenex tissue and encouraged me to just let it out! After regaining my composure, she asked what prompted me to have such an outburst? I told her that was the first time that anyone associated with the medical field had just stated so plainly that Mary only had a 5% chance of surviving. So, me coming in here with my guard down, this was the first-time that I fully acknowledged the seriousness of Mary's diagnosis. She agreed, then asked me how I felt about having had this outburst of emotion? I told her that I thought it was a very good thing spiritually, mentally & physically. That obviously I had a lot of emotion pent up inside that needed to be released. She agreed and proceeded to paint the picture of Mary's present life!

Mary's life has literally been turned upside down! In a matter of a few short weeks, she has been reduced from a very independent self-sufficient woman to a woman who needs assistance with daily routine activities. She has gone from providing care as a caregiver to care being provided for her. She has lost total control of how she has always functioned in life which is a constant reminder of her diagnosis. In my opinion, this is why she is resisting to consume the things that you are providing for her. It's not so much what you're providing or when you're providing it, psychologically, you're attempting to take over the one thing that she is still capable of doing on her own which is to feed herself! This is very normal behavior between spouses given the circumstance. My guidance to you would be to set up an area convenient for Mary to feed herself. Your responsibility then becomes simply to make items available without any commentary, which in turn allows Mary the freedom to feed herself as she wishes. I believe that by doing this, Mary will benefit both mentally and physically, in addition to you being relieved from the frustration and anxiety that you have been experiencing. Does this sound like a plan that interests you? I replied, "yes it does!"

Once returning home, I went in to check on Mary. Fortunately, she was sitting up in bed and curious about the counseling session that I had just returned from. She knew how I felt about that sort of thing and that I was somewhat hesitant about keeping the appointment. I told her that it was amazing and much needed. I explained to her how the counselor was able to provide me with a look behind the curtain into your current life's circumstance. This allowed me to see things from your perspective and not just mine. As I continued to tell Mary about what the counselor believed that she was experiencing, her countenance began to change for the better. She then said that's exactly how it is, but I just didn't know how to express this to you. I told her about setting up an area for her to eat as she felt inclined to. She loved this idea which prompted me to immediately set it up. We thanked God for providing us with insight for such a time as this and for Him to bless the vessel through which it was provided. Once again, He had measured out to us the heavenly attributes that we both needed to sustain us at this time!

After getting Mary settled for the night, I was able to get a night's rest like unable before. I was very thankful for what had transpired the previous day. Once waking the following morning, I got Mary ready and we went for her to get IV fluids for medications and hydration at the Oncologists' facility. While she was receiving her treatment, I spoke with her new best friend about my counseling session the previous day. I told her that it was amazing! That I was very appreciative that she was mindful enough to advise me for this type of counseling. She responded with a smile stating that I've been at this a long time and can tell when someone needs this type of counseling. I thanked her again as Mary, her sister and I departed the facility to head back home.

Once arriving back home and getting settled in, the three of us were in a very good frame of mind. So much so that instead of Mary settling in the bedroom, she wanted to settle in the rec room with her sister and I to watch some TV for the evening. This is one of those moments that I will always cherish. Just glancing at Mary across the room, she looked like her old self! That she had no deadly diagnosis whatsoever. I'm typically a very positive person. But you know that old saying! Sometimes, beware of the calm before the storm because the calm indicates that the storm is on the horizon. Unfortunately, this would be the case in just a matter of a handful of hours. The three of us would be introduced to new territory like never before on this journey that we found ourselves going through.

After watching TV for a few hours, I helped Mary to the hall bathroom to start the process to go to sleep for the evening. I left her unassisted on the toilet, which was a routine thing to do while I went to get her medications from the rec room. While in the rec room getting her medications, I heard a thud! I immediately ran to the hall bathroom and Mary had fell off the toilet and was laying on the floor wedged between the toilet and the bathtub. I shouted, oh my God! I immediately knelt, checked her out, and assisted her back up onto the toilet. She stated, I don't know what happened. I was just sitting there and the next thing I remember is that I'm lying on the floor. I checked her out even better when she was sitting on the toilet. She had a red mark on her right side where it hit against the bathtub but there were no abrasions or broken bones.

Her sister and I assisted her to the bedroom to sit on the edge of the bed. Other than being shaken up, she seemed to be in relatively good shape. I had taken her vital signs which were all normal but to be on the safe side, I called the nurses hotline for assistance. After giving all the pertinent information to the nurse on call, she concurred with the decision to allow Mary to go to sleep under one condition. Keep an eye on her throughout the night and if anything of concern arises, immediately call an ambulance. I told her I would and that we appreciated the service they provide 24/7.

Typically, when Mary would go to sleep, I would usually stay up for a couple of hours to try to unwind. Also, I'm a very loud snorer which unfortunately keeps her awake if I were to fall asleep prior to her. Not tonight! Because of this evenings' events, I just wanted to be with her throughout the night, holding her close being attentive to her needs. It would be one of those night's where the Lord touched me to be relaxed and restored without necessarily sleeping. It's hard to explain but He thankfully has touched me several times in this manner throughout my life when most needed. After what turned out to be 6 or 7 hours later, Mary said that she couldn't move her legs. I immediately called an ambulance!

Once arriving at the medical facility, I knew that Mary would be in good hands. This is the same facility that houses Mary's oncologist office. They know the drill when a cancer patient arrives. The protocol that is to be followed concerning a patient currently being treated for cancer. They immediately transported her to a private room with a nurse drawing her blood. The nurse then proceeded to set up an IV as to administer fluids. In what seemed like no time at all, the doctor arrived with his diagnosis. The test results revealed that Mary had an excessive amount of pain medication in her bloodstream. Unfortunately, due to the cancer, Mary's liver was unable to process the pain medication properly. The plan is to flood Mary's body with IV fluids as to flush out her system. The doctor believed that once this was accomplished, Mary would regain use of her legs. He planned on keeping her throughout the weekend for her condition to stabilize, and to have the opportunity to readjust her pain medications in agreement with her Oncologist. I thanked him for taking such good care of her.

It took three or four hours to totally flush Mary's system out. As the doctor had hoped for, and we were praying for, Mary regained use of her legs. We were just thanking and praising God for his goodness in that moment. Once a room became available, they transported Mary to a private room at the hospital. Unbeknownst to us at the time, Mary would be spending five of the next seven weeks of her life here. As always, when Mary would have an episode, we would contact family and friends. On this occasion, two of Mary's brothers were able to come from out of town and spend some time with her this Saturday evening. Once they saw their sister and recognized her loss of weight, they became concerned as was everyone else about her lack of eating. I pulled both of them to the side and relayed the message that the grief counselor had told me. Do not try to force her into eating or it'll make her withdraw even more. They acknowledged that they understood.

With Mary having three of her siblings there to visit, I saw it as an opportunity for me to go to our home and sort through some business. For the past month or so, I had just allowed the mail to pile up on the kitchen counter and would deal with it later. Later was now. Having retired from the Postal Service after 31 years. Management always frowned upon the use of the term junk mail. However, in this moment, I found myself sorting through a lot of junk mail which immediately found its way to the bottom of the trash can. After dealing with the relevant mail, I threw a load of clothes in the washer and got something to eat.

As I sat there eating, I started to reflect on things. This was the first time since Mary's diagnosis that I found myself home alone. While I openly confess to being the ultimate homebody, I did not like being home alone in this moment. I believe it was because this was a precursor of things to come. Deep down, at some point, Mary was going to die, and this was going to be my future. My imagination started running away with me. I simply could not envision myself being single at the age of 60. I love being married. I enjoy being married. I found comfort in being blessed with a great marriage. It's all I had known for the last 35 plus years, and I feared the jeopardy of it being taken away from me. At that moment, the washing machines timer sounded off which immediately brought me out of my stupor.

After throwing the clothes in the dryer, I walked around the house just praying in the spirit and talking to the Lord. It never ceases to amaze me, how when we call out for the Lord's help, He responds immediately. He may not change the circumstance as we had hoped or prayed for, but he always provides what we need to sustain us in spite of the circumstance. The fear that I was struggling with just moments earlier had dissipated. Once again, my Lord had comforted me with that peace that passes all understanding. After thanking God for His goodness, His kindness, and His mercy, I walked back to the kitchen area of the house. I then realized that the clothes had finished drying. After folding and hanging clothes, I headed back to the hospital.

Once returning to Mary's room, I was greeted with a great deal of enthusiasm. Evidently, in my absence, Mary had found her appetite and consumed quite a bit of food. This was awesome! She seemed to be in good spirits and was very talkative with her siblings. Unfortunately, our celebration would be short lived. Within the hour, she would regurgitate everything that she had consumed. This caused a great deal of concern, primarily with the stent that had been implanted in her small intestine. Was it still functioning properly so that her digestive system could process food properly? This prompted the doctor to set up a test which would answer this very question. Fortunately, he was able to set up this test for the next morning even though it would be on a Sunday. Mary's brothers said their goodbyes and we settled in for the night.

It's almost impossible to get a good night's rest in a hospital. At least it is for me anyway. You've got the constant comings and goings of the medical staff, the beeping of machines but mainly the lack of comfort that you're accustomed to having in your own home. All this combined with the concern that you have for your wife, it's a tall order to attempt to calm your mind to the point of getting any rest. Nonetheless, by God's goodness, He always seemed to sustain me through this season regardless of circumstances. As I was hoping and praying that Mary would have a good report on her test the following day, I dozed off until awakened by medical staff bright and early.

Fortunately, Mary wasn't feeling nauseous this morning in spite of her episode from the previous night. For the test to be conducted properly, she would have to drink a good amount of contrast to highlight if her digestive system was flowing properly. To conduct the test, she was strapped to a table which was attached to a conveyor system. I must admit that the appearance of this contraption was somewhat amusing as long as I wasn't the one strapped to it. This, along with the fact that Mary was having a blast on this thing regardless of the position in which they had her in. At one point, they had her suspended approximately 8 feet off the floor horizontally with her facing downward! She literally shouted, "boy, I bet you can't find this ride at Disney World!" Honestly, it was quite entertaining for all parties involved. The medical staff were touched by her carefree attitude and infectious laughter, plus I loved seeing the childlike joy radiating from within her very being. This is what had first drawn me to her when we met over 36 years ago!

Once the entertainment had concluded, the test results revealed that the stent was doing its job and that her digestive tract was functioning but at a slower rate than normal due to continued healing. The final diagnosis was that she had simply consumed her meal at a more rapid pace than what her system could keep up with. Lesson learned!

More is not always better especially when you're going through a healing process. We thanked God that everything was functioning and would get better over time. I can't tell you how many times over the past 4 plus years that I've reflected on the joy that was provided while Mary went through this test. It brings a smile to my face every time and is possibly my favorite memory of her while going through this season!

Now that we're comfortably back in Mary's room with a good report, it's time to have a consultation with her doctor to start talking about being discharged. She begins her radiation treatment tomorrow at noon, which will last for the entire week. She also has an appointment on Friday after her final radiation treatment to have a port installed to begin chemotherapy treatment the following week. With this in mind, her doctor would only release her under one condition. That I would be capable of giving her blood thinner shots into her abdominal area. I responded, "sure, just show me how to do it." He promptly had a nurse come in to give me a brief tutorial and allowed me to give Mary a blood thinner shot. With all parties feeling comfortable with the procedures in place, we filled out the necessary paperwork and started our merry way home.

After arriving home and getting settled for the night, Mary and I had one of our best conversations during this journey. For starters, we didn't know if we would make it to this point! We knew that time was of the essence, so we both were just hoping and praying that Mary's overall physicality would remain intact to go through treatment. Even though her digestive system was still in a healing process and she was down 10 to 15 pounds. She had a very strong heart and set of lungs plus, she was in a very positive frame of mind. We both just thanked God for getting her to this point! We thanked him in advance for measuring out to her all the provision that she would require to receive her healing and to get through treatment if needed. We both at this point were getting somewhat comfortable with just staying in the moment and thanking God for what he had provided. Scripture tells us to walk by faith, not by sight. So, we would just continue to take it one day at a time by walking through the door/doors that would be necessary for Mary to receive her healing.

CHAPTER EIGHT
TREATMENT

Thankfully by God's grace, we've made it to treatment week. Mary is scheduled to have radiation treatments Monday thru Friday at noon this week. The plan is to bombard the perimeter of the tumor for five consecutive days as to deaden it preventing any future growth. Succeeded by 12 weeks of chemotherapy to destroy any cancer cells that had spread throughout Mary's body. We both had known and knew of people who had received these types of treatment, but this would be a brand-new experience for the two of us. We had been well informed about the potentially detrimental side effects from both types of treatment. This prompted us to pray accordingly, "Lord, we continue to thank you and praise you for Mary's healing! We acknowledge that your ways are higher than ours and while we don't always understand the path that you have prepared before us; we thank you for binding any dangerous side effects from these treatments in Jesus' name, amen!"

The routine for the next 5 days would be to leave home by 1130 to arrive at the treatment facility by 1150 for scheduled treatment at 12. Typically, by the time I dropped Mary and her sister off at the entrance and found a parking space, as I was walking towards the entrance they would be walking back out. Her treatment sessions only lasted for about 15 minutes with the facility operating like clockwork! The only day this week that I actually went inside for any length of time was on Friday which was to go over any post treatment instructions and sign the necessary paperwork for discharge from radiation treatment.

After Mary was discharged from her final radiation treatment, we immediately headed to outpatient admitting at the hospital next door. Mary had to have a port surgically implanted in her upper chest area to better accommodate for chemotherapy treatments.
It was a procedure that would take less than an hour which would work perfectly to get Mary back home prior to Friday rush hour traffic. Thankfully, the port was installed without complications however, Mary did experience some nauseousness resulting in her vomiting prior to being discharged. I always felt so bad for her having to experience these episodes of sickness. Fortunately, she fell asleep during the short ride home and we were able to beat rush hour traffic as well.

Once getting Mary inside and getting her settled in our bedroom, she immediately fell back to sleep. This was pretty much commonplace for this entire week. Each day seemed exactly the same (which they pretty much were), and the week sped by in a blur! Daily, after getting Mary back home and settled, I would administer any medications while making an assortment of proteins available for her to consume as she felt led. It was very important that she stay hydrated and maintain her weight going into chemotherapy which begins the following Wednesday. She had done very well this week by ending with the same weight as she had begun.

With phase one of treatment behind us, I went outside on our covered deck to somewhat remove myself from the circumstance. As I reflected on the previous 2 months (which felt like 2 years), I suddenly slumped onto the table and started sobbing for several minutes. Once I had composed myself, I felt like a heavy weight had been lifted! That I had been recentered spiritually, mentally and physically. I began to thank God for all that He had done in my life! How He had prepared my heart to receive Jesus as my Lord and Saviour shortly before my 23rd birthday. How He supernaturally delivered me from drugs and alcohol that same day prior to Mary's and mine paths crossing 11 months later.

You see, when I was 16, I started drinking alcohol and smoking pot occasionally. When I failed to make the high school baseball team as a sophomore, it shook the very foundation of my life! I always believed that I would play centerfield for the New York Yankees. When I was 6 months old, I was nicknamed Mickey after my father's favorite baseball player at the time, Mickey Mantle. My father was very athletic and had lettered in baseball, football, basketball and track in high school. He would spend several hours throughout my childhood teaching my younger brother and I the basic fundamentals of these sports but primarily focused on baseball. So, when I failed to make the high school team, I felt like I had let my father down and I allowed a wall to separate me from his presence. In essence, I was preventing him from being a father to me when I most needed it. It was at this point in my life when I removed myself from any kind of athletics and immersed myself in school (as needed), but mainly working and music. Music had replaced the void in my life left by the removal of athletics. I started attending an abundant amount of rock concerts and could identify with Mick Jagger of the Rolling Stones more so than I could Mickey Mantle of the New York Yankees.

I continued this lifestyle for the remainder of high school and throughout my first 2 years of college. Outwardly, I could present that all was well in the situations in which it was required but internally I was a miserable person. Behind closed doors I was mad at the world! I had always believed in God but now I was starting to question Him about things more than I ever had before. We attended church as a family until my paternal grandmother died in 1968 when I was 11 years old. Her death prompted me to really have conversations with God at bedtime after we had said our nightly prayers. I wanted to see my mamaw again, so I was asking God what I needed to do for this to happen. I knew it had something to with Jesus and being born again but it just didn't make any sense to me.

So, then I find myself 9 years later at the age of 20 wondering how my life ended up here! It couldn't be my fault based on the decisions that I had made over the last few years, it had to be the world's fault! It was the world's fault that I was drinking alcohol and smoking pot on pretty much a daily basis. It was the world's fault that I didn't make the baseball team in high school which prompted this downward spiral. It was the world's fault that my college advisor had suggested that I change majors to have better employment opportunities. So, I concluded that since everything in my life was the world's fault, that I simply needed to live in another part of the world because I had to be living in the wrong part for my life to be so messed up. My solution was to join the Army!

I started active duty in the U.S. Army on May 25, 1977. I would be assigned to Fort Jackson South Carolina for basic training approximately 3 months before being reassigned to Fort Lee Virginia for Advanced Individual Training for another 2 months. Once completing both of these assignments, I would be transferred to Schofield Barracks Hawaii for 31 months to complete my 3 years of enlistment. The first 5 months of my enlistment went according to plan. During basic training you were isolated from any type of alcohol or drugs. In AIT you had more freedom which provided some access to alcohol, but I had no interest. So, I was off and running towards sobriety and it was all because I had changed my location in the world!

I arrived at Schofield Barracks Hawaii in October 1977. Ever since I was in grade school I wanted to go to Hawaii. That is when I first saw a picture of Diamond Head rising above in the background of Waikiki Beach. The plane touched down at Hickam Air Force Base at approximately 4 a.m. The temperature was 72 degrees and I had started a season of winterless life that would last for 3 years. We were loaded up on a deuce and a half truck which transported us to our duty assignments at Schofield Barracks. I was assigned to the Maintenance Platoon, HHC 65th Combat Engineer Battalion.

Now that I had reached the permanent party stage of my military career, I had a lot more leeway as to how I spent my time off. You had the freedom to do as you please as long as you were back to make formation and any assignments. I did well concerning not putting myself in any compromising situations pertaining to sobriety and my new way of life until an incident with a M-60 tank sounding off occurred May 1978. The compression of the blast knocked 2 fellow soldiers and me to the ground with our heads pounding and our ears ringing. It was about this same time that I incurred a separate injury that would require surgery a few months later. It was during this season that I began to drink alcohol again and started smoking pot on occasion. I've always been dedicated to my assignments and/or responsibilities and was always in a sober frame of mind at these times. Unfortunately, while off duty, I found myself back to where I was prior to enlisting in the Army. My plan was falling apart, and the only common denominator was me!

At this point, I still had 2 more years of service to complete. While outwardly I was receiving my fair share of awards, commendations and promotions; inwardly I was even more miserable and frustrated because I knew that relocation was not the answer. I knew that I had a void, an emptiness in my life and I didn't know how to fill it! I had sought spiritual help during basic training pertaining to salvation, but the demands of the chaplain left another and me walking away. The chaplain stated that to achieve salvation, one had to accept Jesus as Saviour, be baptized, and get 3 people to do the same. I disagreed with the third requirement so as stated earlier two of us walked away.

So, over the next 21 months I continued to live this way of life. At one point, I found myself in the spur of the moment at a party snorting some cocaine. My heart started beating so rapidly to the point that I thought I was going to die. I put on Stairway to Heaven, lay down on my bed and prayed to God that He wouldn't let me die at the age of 22. Thankfully He honored this request! It was at this point that I bottomed out and started sincerely seeking God for help. My parents around Christmas of 1979 had accepted Jesus and had sent me a care package containing a family bible along with 2 tracts of scripture pertaining to salvation in Jesus. I had kept these items in a tin container under my bed but had recently moved them to my nightstand for daily reading.

It was around this time that the Holy Spirit was really preparing my heart to accept Jesus as Saviour. Training exercises were really ramping up and everyone living off base had to stay on base due to the Iranian hostage situation. I remember being in formation one day when that still small voice inside asked me where I would go if I were to die right now. My response was to hell! Unfortunately, He confirmed that. I responded with I don't know what to do that seems to be legit. Every avenue I've pursued someone seems to be adding their own traditions or list of requirements. Please God! Send someone my way to present your truth! Not their truth or someone else's truth, but your truth!

Bob Dylan had released his first Christian album Slow Train Coming. This album was a godsend in my life! It was the kind of music that I loved to listen to along with scriptural lyrics from the Bible. As I would sing along with each song (unbeknownst to me at the time), I was sowing God's word into the very fabric of my being! The internal heaviness that I had been experiencing for 6 to 7 years was beginning to dissipate. Spiritually, I knew that help was on the way, that my salvation was near! I had a heightened sense of expectation like never before. The only question was how and when!

It's now approximately 6 weeks later, Valentine's Day 1980. As excited as I was about my salvation 6 weeks ago, I've really been struggling as of late. I thought that I would have been saved by now. I don't know exactly what it is that I need to get me over the hump, but I thought it would have happened by now. Because we had recently passed our annual Inspector General's evaluation, we were authorized to knock off half a day early and have a celebration in the park on base across from the motor pool. Beer was provided and even though I felt that I was growing spiritually, I continued to drink alcohol and smoke pot occasionally. After we had been celebrating for about an hour, we were informed that a special dignitary would be speaking at the base chapel. Since the base chapel was located right across from the park, our presence was required to pack the house for this guest speaker. So, we tidied ourselves up and walked across the street to pack the house as ordered.

Once inside, we were informed that the guest speaker would be former NASA astronaut Jim Irwin. I just shook my head and thought, God, can things get any worse? I'm sitting here half lit in a church, feeling guilty, confused, and now I must against my will, listen to a national hero talk about how all his dreams have been fulfilled! I looked to see if there was any way that I could slip out but that wasn't an option as Military Police were literally posted at each exit for the security of the high-ranking officials within. Surprisingly, once I accepted the circumstance in which I found myself, I asked God to forgive me for being somewhat inebriated in His house. As I silently finished this confession, Mr. Irwin was being introduced to the podium.

When Mr. Irwin approached the podium, he was nothing in appearance that I had anticipated. I was expecting a big, strapping, athletic astronaut type but, he was of average height and seemed somewhat frail in nature. After he had introduced himself, he confirmed my observation by stating that he was probably not in appearance what we all had expected. While he was only approaching 50 years in age, he had struggled with severe heart issues associated with his time in 0-gravity while in space. Instead of feeling envious and somewhat jealous of this man, I suddenly felt very empathetic towards him. From this point forward he had my undivided attention. Little did I realize; this was the beginning of my prayer for salvation being manifested in my life.

Mr. Irwin proceeded to confess how his obsession with being an astronaut had resulted in divorce in his first marriage. He continued to reveal how he had a training accident which nearly resulted in a leg being amputated. To cope with the pain he was experiencing, he chose to mix alcohol with the prescribed pain medication. He was missing in action as both a husband and a father along with the fact that he was mad at the world (sound like someone else) for his dream of becoming an astronaut was fading fast. With his marriage on the rocks and the end of his career in sight, He felt helpless and hopeless! When suddenly, he received a phone call from an old friend.

Mr. Irwin hadn't heard from this friend in years. His friend told him that the Lord had impressed upon his heart to call him and invite him to church that night. Mr. Irwin told him that while I haven't been to church in years, I need to try something because my life is literally falling apart as we speak. While at church that night, Mr. Irwin confessed how it seemed as if the sermon had been tailored made for him. How every syllable of God's living word was washing away the pain, the hurt, the bitterness and the addictions that had somehow consumed his life. When suddenly, he found himself at altar call wanting to receive Jesus as Lord and Saviour. He said the minister told him that all he had to do to receive his salvation was, "to confess with your mouth Jesus as Lord, and believe in your heart that God raised Him from the dead, you will be saved." (NASB, Romans 10:9) Mr. Irwin continued to testify how he became a new creation in Christ Jesus that evening. How old things had passed away and that he was delivered and set free of any addictions in that moment. At this point I was in tears and inwardly my spirit was shouting out, "that's what I've been looking for!"

Mr. Irwin continued to tell us how even though his life is far from perfect. Since Jesus came into his life, his marriage was restored, he passed astronaut training on his final attempt and was accepted into the Apollo program. However, the biggest change in his life was the freedom that he had in Jesus! He was no longer in any kind of bondage and he could sense the presence of God. This presence of God was strongest felt when he was on the surface of the moon. While driving on the moon in the lunar rover, the Holy Spirit impressed upon Mr. Irwin that God wanted to put things into perspective for him. So, when he arrived at a certain viewpoint, the Holy Spirit had Mr. Irwin hold his hand out as if he was holding the earth in the palm of his hand. Mr. Irwin felt silly but was obedient to the request. In that moment, God put things in perspective. He told Mr. Irwin that while the earth is the size of a ball from where you currently stand, the earth is the size of a pinhead from where I'm sitting on my throne in heaven. Don't ever doubt that I can remove anything in your life that seems insurmountable!

Just like Mr. Irwin felt like the sermon that harvested his salvation was tailor made for him, I knew that Mr. Irwin's testimony had been tailor made to harvest my salvation. As he spoke about what God had done and was doing in his life, God's living word was washing away the things in my life that were holding me captive. After Mr. Irwin's presentation, I went forward to thank him for his obedience in sharing his testimony. I told him how I struggled with similar addictions but believed by days end my salvation would be in hand. He graciously thanked me and personally autographed a picture of him standing on the moon, "To. Michael, in His love, Jim Irwin."

Once leaving the post chapel, we were dismissed for the remainder of the day. As I drove to my home off base, I was talking to God reflecting over what had just been revealed to me. I was like, "Lord, is it really that simple to receive my salvation? Simply quote Romans 10:9!" He replied with, "it's more than just quoting it. You have to really believe in your heart that Jesus is Lord and that I raised Him from the dead before you can confess with your mouth that He is Lord. For out of the abundance of the heart, the mouth speaketh (KJV, Matthew 12:34)." For the first time in my life, I had a peace about accepting Jesus as Saviour. Once I arrived home, I read the tract booklet that my parents had sent, In Him." I got down on my knees and confessed all my sins to God. I then recited the Sinner's Prayer in the back of the booklet which included Romans 10:9. I continued to ask God to make me a new creation in Christ Jesus and deliver me from any addictions. The Holy Spirit took residence in my heart at that moment manifesting all that God had in store for me in Christ Jesus! I indeed had been born again and began my new life as a Christian.

I met Mary 11 months later in January 1981 at our church bowling league. She refused to go out with me initially because I was 2 years younger than her. A couple of months later when she found out that I had been stationed in Hawaii, she became somewhat intrigued (or was it Hawaii). She also had wanted to go to Hawaii after seeing a picture of Diamond Head in the background of Waikiki Beach in grade school. So, she agreed to meet me at Shoney's after church for lunch the following Sunday on one condition: That I bring along all my pictures of Hawaii. After we ate and began looking at pictures, she welcomed me to sit next to her as to narrate each picture. By the end of picture gazing, she was holding my hand and we both saw something there in one another's eyes. That unseen, intangible force that resonates in your spirit, I know that I know that this is the person I'm to marry! After 13 months of courtship, we were married April 2, 1982.

So, after 35 years and 7 months of marriage, the woman whose heart is spiritually intertwined with mine is fighting for her life and my Heavenly Father is encouraging me to prepare for life without her! I don't want to Lord! I don't want her to die! I want you to heal her so we can travel together and watch our grandkids grow up! She's only been retired 11 months and deserves to enjoy a much longer retirement! While I continued to plead my case to the Lord, my sister-in-law came out on the deck to let me know that Mary had woke up and wanted me. The timing of her notifying me was a blessing because I was starting to get all worked up and anxious. Our former Pastor always said that God is never late but He's seldom ever early either. His timing is always perfect! At that moment the Holy Spirit comforted me with a verse of scripture that the Lord had impressed upon me when I retired, "be still and know that I am God! I will be exalted among the nations, I will be exalted in the earth." (NKJV, Psalms 46:10)

As I entered the bedroom to check on Mary, she was sitting up in bed with her hand over her shoulder/chest area where the port had been implanted. She said that she was beginning to feel pain as the anesthesia was beginning to wear off. After giving her some medication to help alleviate the pain, she said that while she was clear minded that we needed to have another serious conversation. I knew in my spiwhat the brunt of the conversation would be about since the Holy Spirit had just impressed upon me earlier on the deck to prepare for a life without Mary in it. Not surprisingly, she began by saying that we really needed to start making arrangements as best as possible and that I needed to prepare for living a life without her. I told her that I'm aware of that, so I retrieved pen and paper to write down her requests.

She proceeded to tell me that her first desire was for God to totally heal and restore her to live another 30 years or so. I replied to her that that was my hope and prayer as well. She continued by saying that regardless of how strong my faith is, I sense in my spirit that the answer to my first request is going to be no. She further stated that I don't understand it! It goes against everything that I have an understanding of biblically! No matter how I slice it or dice it, I sense in my spirit that I'm being prepared to transition from the physical realm to the spiritual realm! I just want you to know that these almost 37 years together have been the most wonderful years of my life! That God has truly blessed me abundantly above anything I could ask for or imagine (NIV, Ephesians 3:20). That if I do die, that I'm prepared and ready to go, but I'm concerned about you!

As deep as a conversation as this was, in that moment, I had a sense of peace that can only be provided by the ultimate Comforter, God's Holy Spirit! (KJV, John 14:26) I proceeded to tell Mary how I was going through the same process. That no matter how I prayed or believed according to scripture, that the answer to my request for her to be healed was no! How right out of the gate I asked God, this is not going to turn out the way I want it to is it? The Holy Spirit responded by impressing upon me, no it's not! So, like you! I don't understand why God is allowing this to happen, but now I take comfort in the fact that the two of us are evenly yoked in the Lord while going through this circumstance that we never saw coming!

At this point, Mary and I were bonded together in a way like never before. We got down to the business of what kind of funeral she wanted, where she wanted it, who she wanted to officiate her funeral and who to sing at her funeral. In a strange way, it seemed as if we were planning a long vacation as we had done a few times before throughout the years. I guess the reality of it is there's a lot of truth in that. The only difference being that it's a trip for one with the one left behind to take the same journey also in God's timing. She then questioned me about medical expenses and I comforted her by saying that God was providing as he always does. I asked her if she still wanted to proceed with chemotherapy which would start the following Wednesday and she said that she did. That she still had peace about the treatment plan in place until she didn't. It was time to call it a night! What a day it had been as we drifted asleep embraced in each other's arms.

As was often the case since Mary's diagnosis, a mountaintop moment such as we had experienced the night before, would oftentimes be followed by a very trying or detrimental moment or period of time. Unfortunately, this would hold true for the next handful of days leading into Mary beginning chemotherapy treatments the following Wednesday. Originally, her Oncologist wanted to begin treatment on Tuesday, November 7th but we informed him that that would be her 63rd birthday, so he changed the beginning of treatment to November 8th. During this period of time Mary experienced severe abdominal cramping, pain, nausea, headaches and vomiting. To say the least, she had little or no appetite during this timeframe which resulted in her losing 8 to 10 pounds prior to beginning chemotherapy treatment. She had done so well by maintaining her weight throughout radiation treatment week, which had increased our hope that she would gain weight as opposed to losing weight leading into chemotherapy. Of course, this loss of weight heightened our level of concern!

We had plans for our children and their families to come over on Sunday, November 5th to celebrate Mary's birthday. This day would be more convenient as opposed to trying to pull this event off on her actual birthday which would be a scheduled workday for our children's families. When I reminded Mary that we would be celebrating her birthday today, she said that we needed to reschedule because she didn't feel like having company today. This was an immediate indicator as to how bad this very social and sanguine woman was feeling. I promised her that if she didn't want company that we would figure something out. Thankfully, she began to feel better and wanted to give it a try because she really did want to see everyone especially the grandkids. As I reminisce about that day, I'm so thankful that it happened! There were pictures taken and memories provided that will last a lifetime for my family and me

Well, we have finally made it to chemotherapy treatment day. It's been a little over 5 weeks since Mary had the stent implanted in her duodenum which is within the timeframe planned on. Once we arrived at the treatment facility, they immediately weighed Mary and realized that she had lost 10 pounds since her last visit on Friday. We proceeded to tell the Oncologist and his staff how the last few days have been about as bad as it gets concerning Mary's health. Despite Mary's loss of weight, we all agreed that we should proceed with treatment beginning immediately due to time being of the essence. Since we had been properly educated on the potential detrimental side effects of chemotherapy, Mary, her sister and I joined in prayer to bind those side effects in the name of Jesus and that the treatment would obliterate any cancerous cells in the name of Jesus as well. At this time, they hooked up the treatment tube to Mary's port and her first chemotherapy treatment commenced.

Mary's treatment would last approximately 3 - 4 hours that day in house. Prior to being discharged from treatment, the Oncologist would attach a fanny pack of sorts which would provide an additional 48 hours of treatment while in the comfort of our home. We would then return to the facility to have the treatment pack removed 2 days later on Friday, November 10th with a follow-up appointment scheduled on Wednesday, November 15th. The game plan was to have 6 – 12 bi-weekly treatments dependent upon how Mary responded to the treatments. Unfortunately, when we returned for the follow-up appointment on Wednesday, Mary's bloodwork revealed that her platelet count had dropped to 13 while the scales indicated that she had lost another 12 pounds. Due to this negative report, the Oncologist stated that it's time to discuss what options are available as to plan an alternate course of action.

He stated that due to Mary's overall lack of physicality, he would be postponing any further chemo treatments until she was physically capable of tolerating such treatment. The plan that he had in mind would require hospitalization to address both the low platelet count and loss of weight issues. He would order a series of platelet transfusions to hopefully increase and stabilize Mary's platelet count. This would happen over the next few days. To address the weight loss, he would start Mary on a Total Parenteral Nutrition program or TPN for short to supply her body with nutrition intravenously. TPN had to be initiated while in the hospital but could later be administered at home if hospitalization was not warranted for any other reason. He explained that while there was the potential for unpromising side effects, unfortunately, from a medical perspective, these were the only options available. Mary and I agreed that we were on board which prompted the Oncologist to admit her to the hospital side of the facility. Little did we know, that when we left home at noon today, Mary would never physically set foot in our home again!

CHAPTER NINE
LIFE IN THE HOSPITAL

Once Mary was assigned a room and settled in, I headed home to pick up a few items that she would need over the next handful of days during her stay. The gameplan was to start transfusions on Thursday which would hopefully increase her platelet count and to begin TPN on Friday to address her loss of weight. If everything proceeds as planned, Mary would be back home by noon on Monday. The transfusions were promptly started on Thursday morning as planned as was the TPN on the following morning. Her progress was monitored throughout the weekend with her Oncologist concluding on Monday morning that she needed more transfusions due to her platelet level not meeting goal.

Due to her platelet count being so low, her blood would not properly clot which prompted the Oncologist to drastically reduce the dosage of Mary's blood thinner medication upon admission to the hospital. Unfortunately, one of the side effects of chemotherapy is that it can significantly increase the chance of blood clots forming leading to stroke(s). Sadly, this would be the case later that Monday night at approximately 10 P.M. I was preparing to go home for the evening when suddenly Mary's body jolted upwards from the bed as her vital signs went through the roof! As the medical staff entered the room, they promptly ushered Mary's sister and I out into the hallway. After waiting 15 minutes or so, the doctor informed us that Mary was stable however, she had suffered a stroke and he had ordered a series of tests to determine the extent. It would be a couple of hours before we could see her, so he recommended that we get some coffee in the cafeteria.

After Mary's sister and I had gotten coffee and found a table. She immediately initiated conversation. She promptly told me that I still needed to go home as planned that night and that I needed to see my primary care doctor tomorrow as well. I responded with I know that I need to but I'm not leaving until I get to see her. I believe the both of us were experiencing a certain degree of shock due to Mary having had a stroke. Despite that, we both prayed that the effects would be of no serious consequence and for the Holy Spirit to manifest healing along with comfort to her body. After a couple of hours as promised, we were allowed to check in on her. She was sound asleep! I felt impressed to lay my hands on her and pray in the Spirit. Once I finished, I said my goodbyes and headed home to hopefully get some rest.

Thankfully, I was able to get a good night's rest. However, I hadn't been feeling very well for a few days which is why my sister-in-law reminded me the previous night to see my primary care physician. After getting coffee, I called to make an appointment but could not get one until the following Monday due to this being Thanksgiving week. So, I decided to go to an Urgent Care facility that I had previously went to on occasion. Fortunately, I was able to walk in and within 15 minutes was able to see the staff doctor whom I had seen previously. She and I had developed somewhat of an acquaintanceship over the past 4 years due to the both of us being Christians.

When she walked into the room to greet me, she immediately gasped when she saw my appearance. She reacted with, "oh my God! What is going on Michael?" I became very emotional! On the verge of tears, I informed her that Mary was battling cancer and that despite our faith, I don't think she is going to make it! Being the professional that she is, she proceeded to look over my vitals and other pertinent information gathered and transcribed upon my arrival. She then gave me a good look over before concluding that I had a bad case of pneumonia. After having the nurse give me a couple of shots, she went over the treatment plan which included a 10-day round of antibiotics and returning in 2 weeks for a follow-up appointment.

Once I checked out, she took a break and we had a heart-to-heart conversation. She voiced her concern about my overall health. She stated that if you don't take care of yourself, you will not be able to take care of Mary. I know this is easier said than done but you've lost almost 30 pounds. I told her that I thought I was taking care of myself, but I guess the stress of it all is getting the best of me. She then said that I need to tell you something that you're not going to want to hear but it would be wise to follow this advice. You don't need to be around Mary for the next few days while you're being treated for pneumonia. Her immunity has been compromised due to her treatment and she doesn't need to be exposed to any potential germs. I told her that I understood and that I appreciated her honesty and concern. She then prayed for both Mary and I before I departed stating thank you for the encouragement and I'll see you in a couple of weeks.

As soon as I entered my vehicle to head towards the hospital, I received a call from Mary's sister. She was calling to check on me but more importantly, she said that there was someone who wanted to talk to me, it was Mary! I became very emotional! You see, last I heard, Mary was still asleep and my mind had been going crazy about whether she could talk or what she would be capable of doing. Once I heard her voice, it was both comforting and unsettling. It was comforting to hear her voice and that she could talk, but the way in which she spoke was unsettling because you could tell that the stroke had affected her motor skills. I told her that I would see her soon, that I loved her and that I needed to talk to her sister.

I proceeded to tell my sister-in-law that I had been diagnosed with pneumonia and that I had been advised not to be around Mary due to her immunity being compromised. I asked her to speak with the Oncologist to see if he would allow me to put on a mask to bring her personal items in plus speak to her from a distance. He said that would be fine if I masked up, kept my distance and stayed no longer than 15 minutes. As I entered Mary's room, I noticed that she was sitting up in bed. This was an incredibly good sign! Once our eyes met, her face immediately lit up and she exclaimed, "you're my husband and I've been praying for you." I said, "yes I am! Thank you very much. You're my wife and I've been praying for you too!" She then replied, "yes I am! You're very goodlooking!" I replied, "you're biased!" We then erupted into laughter! Despite the stroke, it was a blessing to know that Mary's sense of humor was still intact!

Once the 15 minutes had expired, Mary and I blew each other kisses goodbye as her sister followed me out to the hallway. She proceeded to update me on any results from the series of tests that had been conducted. Unfortunately, not only had a brain scan confirmed that Mary had a stroke the previous night, but that she also had had a stroke prior to this one within the last month. Immediately, I thought about the night that Mary had fell off the toilet. That would have been October 27th which would fall within the timeframe of the report. The scan also revealed an area of concern which could possibly be bleeding caused by the stroke/s or brain cancer. The plan concerning this was to do another scan on Friday, the day after Thanksgiving to see if this area had changed in size. On the bright side, thankfully, Mary's platelet count had increased to the point where they could administer heparin by IV to better control the thickness/thinness of her blood to help prevent any future blood clots. She had also gained approximately 5 pounds since beginning TPN treatment the previous Friday. Because of Mary's extended hospital stay, the administrators of TPN suspended the at home treatments which were scheduled to start the previous day. They would continue the treatments in the hospital until further notice. I hugged my sister-in-law bye, thanked her for being here, and headed back home.

As I drove home, my mind was all over the place thinking about what had happened in the past few hours. Once I arrived home, I immediately called my son and daughter to update them on their mother's condition as well as my own. With Thanksgiving being just 2 days away, my daughter had plans to celebrate the holiday out of town with her in-laws, while my son had plans to celebrate the holiday locally with our side of the family at my parents. While speaking with my son, he suggested that after he visited his mom on Wednesday after work, that he would swing by and pick me up to spend the night with his family to go to my parents on Thanksgiving the following day. I told him that I liked the idea, but that it would depend on how I was feeling. I may just have him bring me back a plate on their way back home.

After updating a few more people by phone or text, I collapsed on the bed and just started sobbing for a few minutes. The emotion of everything that was happening just overwhelmed me! The one place that I wanted to be more than anything in the world, I could not be there! I'm Mary's husband! That is my rightful place to be! I totally understood why it was best that I not be there, but knowing that, didn't lessen the pain of not being able to support my wife by her side! Once getting that out of my system, I heated up some soup, poured some ginger ale and retrieved my medications from the kitchen to kick this pneumonia in the tail! At that moment, I realized the best thing that I could do for all concerned was to pray myself to sleep after eating. So that's what I did!

Wow! What a difference a day can make in the Lord! I was blessed with almost 14 hours of sleep! I don't think I've ever slept that long before, well, except for the last time that I was battling pneumonia several years ago. So, I praised the Lord for His goodness, put on a pot of coffee, and called my sister-in-law to check on Mary. I was in a positive mindset and was anticipating a good report.

My sister-in-law indicated that while Mary was sleeping at the moment, she hadn't been as alert as the previous day, that something just seemed to be a little off. She brought this to the medical staff's attention, and they concluded that it was the aftereffects of the stroke. She asked how I was doing, and I told her that I was feeling much better. I informed her that my son would be stopping by later to check on his mom, and to see if they needed anything. I told her to keep me posted if anything changed.

I had a few hours to fill before my son would be stopping by to pick me up. I had already decided to spend the night at his home and had notified him as such. I decided to eat some breakfast, take medications, and to spend some time in the upper room (our rec room). I always felt closest to the Lord when communing with Him in this room. Hence, the nickname. Once I entered the room, I was overwhelmed! There were numerous bottles of medications lined up systematically with post-it-note instructions, a hazmat suit in case a breach occurred during Mary's at home chemo treatment, syringes prefilled with blood thinner medication, and finally instructions on how to properly administer and store the TPN product when Mary came back home. Honestly, in that moment, I fell to my knees and thanked God that Mary was in the care of professionals at the hospital. I also thanked Him for blessing me with the wisdom that I needed to properly administer and provide care for my wife during this season as well.

Once my son arrived, I tossed my bag in the backseat of his truck and we were off to his home. He said that he had a nice visit with his mom. That she was awake and was really glad to see him, but he could tell that the stroke had affected her motor skills. To say the least, we were both very concerned about her. I simply told him that my prayer life had increased tremendously during this season and that my faith was being tested like no other time in my life. That while I was standing on God's promises, I also had this troubling in my spirit that Mary wasn't going to make it. That He was preparing me to let her go and to Apostle Paul it in life until further notice. While I know that this confession saddened us, I just needed to express to my son what I was experiencing. We both got somewhat emotional at this point as we pulled into his driveway.

As we entered my son's home, we were promptly greeted by my almost 16-month-old grandson and their rambunctious boxer named Ellie! They both love their papa! Sometimes I play with Ellie but due to allergies and with me being under the weather, I slid off into my grandson's playroom and dedicated my time to him. He is Mary and mine's first grandchild. We've always loved and enjoyed being around children, that's probably why we always were involved with children's ministries at church. To me, children are the most precious people on the planet. They have that innocence and trust that God instilled when creating mankind in the beginning. Unfortunately, as we go through life, a part of us becomes tainted and we buildup walls that hinder our relationship with not only other people but with God as well. I know I'm guilty of this! As I played with my grandson, the Lord was using this time to keep my mind still where He could perform what I call supernatural surgery upon me. I was being transformed by the renewing of my mind! (NIV, Romans 12:2)

Play hard, sleep hard! My grandson had played himself to sleep so it was time to retire for the evening. My son and daughter-inlaw had set up a room for me to sleep in upstairs. As I lay in bed, I sensed in my spirit that this would be a prelude of my life to come. While I enjoyed being around my children and their families, I didn't like the fact at all of being alone in bed especially not in my own home! However, in that moment, I found myself thanking God for His goodness! Despite being on antibiotics for only 2 days, I felt refreshed and renewed! It was then that I realized that the Lord had touched me while I was playing with my grandson! I then prayed that He would touch Mary in the same way that He had touched me as I drifted off to sleep.

It's Thanksgiving morning and unfortunately, I received a phone call from my sister-in-law at 8:00 a.m. frantically requesting for me to come to the hospital. Once she somewhat settled down, she told me that Mary was in a catatonic state and that the doctor was requesting my presence! That if she was going to respond to anyone at all, that it would probably be me! So, I got dressed and immediately went downstairs to notify my son what was going on. He said to give him time to get dressed because he felt led to go with me.

As we were driving towards the hospital, our route took us through our old stomping grounds. We drove past the bowling alley where Mary and I first met. We drove by the Shoney's where we had our first date looking at the pictures from Hawaii. We drove by the street where we had purchased our first home. We drove by the street where our church that we had first met at had relocated to. We drove by the school that our kids had attended for both elementary and junior high. We drove by numerous restaurants that we had frequented throughout the years. Especially the ones where kids ate free on certain days during the week. It was kind of a "This Is Your Life" moment as we proceeded down memory lane. Surprisingly, instead of becoming saddened by this, the memories brought smiles to both our faces.

Once we had arrived on Mary's floor at the hospital, we were immediately met by her medical physician and her sister. They proceeded to tell us that Mary hadn't responded to anyone or had anything to drink or eat for several hours and was in a somewhat catatonic state. Due to this condition, she was designated NPO (to receive nothing by mouth) until her condition improved and was cleared by the speech therapist to begin oral consumption. Furthermore, she had the appearance of someone who was restrained displaying little or no emotion. So be prepared to be shocked by what you're about to experience. I sighed, "oh, Lord" as I began to pray in the Spirit before donning protective gear and entering her room.

As we entered Mary's room, I noticed that she was laying on her back with her head elevated to a comfortable position. As I walked to the front of Mary's bed directly into her line of sight, she displayed no reaction whatsoever and her eyes appeared to have a layer of film over them. As I seated myself next to her, I instinctively cradled her left hand between my hands. Still no reaction! Not wanting to get too close due to my illness, I slightly leaned in speaking in a soft voice I whispered, "hey baby." She immediately turned her head towards me and whispered, "hey baby" followed by a slight smile. I then asked her how she was feeling? She replied by saying that she had been spending time in the heavenlies with her Heavenly Father. At that point, her medical physician said that it was time for me to leave as he ushered me out.

While my son and sister-in-law stayed a little longer in Mary's room, her medical physician conveyed his preliminary diagnosis with me in the hallway. He stated that he believed that the area of concern in Mary's brain had increased in size which in turn was causing the symptoms in which she was experiencing. He further stated that he had a brain scan scheduled for the following afternoon and would probably have the results the following morning on Saturday. He concluded the conversation by stating that I know you folks are some praying people as is my wife. It's a good thing because we're going to need some help from the Almighty on this one!

As my son and I left the hospital, we promised my sister-in-law, his aunt, that we would bring her by a couple of plates of Thanksgiving food and desserts later that evening. Once arriving at my parents' home for Thanksgiving dinner, I was overwhelmed in a plethora of ways! For starters, I'm not a very social person and have always felt uncomfortable at any gathering despite it being family. In this case, and rightfully so, everyone wanted updates on Mary's condition. So, updating everyone throughout the night, while necessary, was extremely exhausting especially considering my physical, mental and emotional condition.

So, at some point I removed myself from the crowd by going outside for some alone time to compose myself. Occasionally, I had employed this tactic at past gatherings to accommodate my pure melancholy temperament. I would later find out at a Griefshare meeting this tactic was considered to be exercising wisdom when confronted with this situation while grieving. It was wise to have an escape plan so to speak. This course of action worked for a few minutes until the smokers started congregating outside after filling their bellies. I can't handle cigarette smoke, so I made my way back indoors and fortunately spent some time with my parents before we headed back to the hospital to check on Mary and drop off some food.

It's now Saturday morning and my son and I are headed to the hospital to meet with Mary's medical physician to go over the results of the brain scan. It was not good news! Unfortunately, his preliminary diagnosis was confirmed. The area of concern in her brain had enlarged resulting in her current catatonic state. While he suspected cancer was the culprit, the scan revealed a substantial amount of bleeding which somewhat clouded the imaging. Regardless of what was causing her symptoms, due to Mary's overall lack of physicality, the only treatment that could be provided would be to manage her pain, which surprisingly she didn't have any. The physicians' recommendation was to call in hospice care. I immediately started crying on my son's shoulder which prompted the physician to remark, "are you crying?" I replied, "yes, I'm crying! You just gave us the worse news possible, so yes, I'm crying!" He then stated, "men in my country don't cry, especially in public." I concluded by stating, "well then something's seriously wrong with your country" as I walked away.

After I had somewhat composed myself, I returned to join in the conversation that had continued in my absence between the physician, my son and sister-in-law. The physician immediately apologized conveying that it was not his intent to upset me. I accepted his apology while he informed me that a hospice representative would be in house within a couple of hours. As our conversation concluded, I pulled him to the side and told him that I was sorry for the way I reacted to his earlier statement. He put his hand on my shoulder, leaned in and said that while his wife was alive and well, that he had a brother who was fighting for his life. So, I have an understanding when it comes to the emotions attached to potentially losing a family member. As he was walking away, he stopped, turned around and asked if I would lift his brother up in prayer. I told him that I would. From that point forward, whenever our paths crossed at the hospital, we greeted one another with a handshake followed by a hug. God is good!

Once the physician left, my son, sister-in-law and I contacted family members and friends by text or phone to give them the bad report. Of course, since my son was at my side, the hardest call for me to make was to my daughter who was out of town for Thanksgiving. Honestly, now, I can't remember much of what we spoke about.

I just remember a lot of tears being shed with her replying that they would be at the hospital later that day. I do remember saying to her to take your time and be careful. Once the three of us had reached out to everyone that we could think of, we needed to come up with some sort of plan for visitation at the hospital. There were a few of Mary's coworkers who were in from out of town for the holiday who wanted to visit. Also, there were several local relatives and friends who wanted to visit as well. This all had been planned prior to Mary taking a turn for the worse.

We decided that the people who were in from out of town should take priority over the others followed by pastors and those closest to Mary. We notified everyone of our intentions and would play it by ear as to how many visitors to allow throughout the day. The first group consisted of four people that Mary had worked with, one who was her supervisor at one point. I had met him at some work gatherings previously. He and Mary had a very good work relationship and I knew that if all possible, she might respond if he could compose himself long enough to attempt to communicate with her. This would be a tall order! I had tried to prepare everyone for Mary's current condition so they wouldn't be totally caught off guard. So, when he first went in and saw her, he couldn't handle it and bolted out of the room crying. I told him that it was okay whether he wanted to try again or not was strictly up to him. He wanted to and it paid huge dividends. Once he sat by her bedside and whispered who he was, Mary turned her head towards him, smiled and whispered his name. After this happened, we decided to cancel all visitors except for one group coming at 8:00 p.m. that evening. We all needed to try to get some rest. It had been a very emotional day!

After unwinding for a brief period of time, there was a knock on the door of Mary's room. When opening the door, I was pleasantly greeted by two representatives from a local hospice facility. They were both very compassionate and consoling. I can't imagine functioning in the capacity in which they choose to operate, but it was evident from the second we met that this was their calling. After introducing them to my son and sister-in-law, we relocated to a more private area of the hospital. They handed out brochures and proceeded to go over the different levels of care provided and vacancies available at local hospice facilities if we chose the inresidence option. We chose the in-residence option that was located closest to our home. However, this facility would not have a vacancy until Monday which was two days away. Fortunately, with it being the weekend, Mary would be allowed to stay at the hospital until transported to the hospice facility on Monday. We thanked them for their assistance during this most trying time and they replied, "we'll see ya'll on Monday!"

Our daughter and her family arrived later that day. It worked out well with them spending some time with Mary prior to visitors arriving around 8:00 p.m. The group that arrived that evening consisted of two couples who we were very close to at church, and our former Pastor from a church we attended when our kids were baptized. To say the least, they were devastated and overwhelmed with emotion when they saw Mary. Here lay a woman whose countenance typically radiated and glowed, lighting up the area in which she inhabited. This remarkable woman who is my helpmate in life had been reduced to a mere shell of herself by this terrible disease. Despite this, Pastor anointed Mary with oil as we all laid hands on her, praying for her healing (James 5:14-15).

Once everyone had left and the dust had settled following the day's events, Mary's sister exited to her vehicle to call her husband as she had been doing on a nightly basis since she had arrived to help care for her sister. While she was attending to this, I finally had some alone time with Mary for the first time since being notified that hospice needed to be called in. Thankfully, the physicians involved had cleared me to spend as much time with her as I wanted despite me still taking antibiotics for pneumonia. As I took my place at her side, I gently caressed her left hand and whispered, "hey baby." Unfortunately, this time, there was no response! Her eyes were slightly open, instead of a film covering her eyes as previously indicated, her eyes seemed to be covered by scales. Of course, this broke my heart which prompted me to lower my head into my hands and sob like I never have before. I cried out, "God! I'm not ready to let her go yet! I know in my heart that is what you're preparing me for but I'm not ready!" In that moment, I sensed no response from my Heavenly Father. I'd never felt so alone, helpless and vulnerable in my life!

As I stood up to pace around and pray in the Spirit, Mary's sister entered the room. She commented, "you look like you could use a break." I replied, "yes I could." This would also allow her to spend some alone time with her sister. As I was in the elevator headed down to the cafeteria, the Holy Spirit began to comfort me in that still, small voice that resides within. He reminded me that despite how you feel at times, you can't base your Heavenly Father's presence on how you feel! Remember that it's based on what His word says, "Be strong and of good courage, fear not, nor be afraid of them: for the Lord thy God, He it is that doth go with thee; he will not fail thee, nor forsake thee" (Deuteronomy 31:6, KJV). Once again God's timing is perfect! It's important to remember that in our most vulnerable moments in life that God in His sovereignty measures out opportunities for our faith to grow. Ironically, for all places for God to minister to me this time was in an elevator! Due to trauma incurred during military service, I can't stand to be in enclosed spaces. I believe that was the point. He will never leave us or forsake us, especially in times when we are most vulnerable or fearful!

CHAPTER TEN
WE GOT A MIRACLE!

At some point during the night, Mary's sister and I had fallen asleep in our respective recliners. It had been 12 days since Mary had been admitted to the hospital. You kind of get use to the comings and goings of medical personnel throughout the night and catch some sleep whenever you can. We were pretty much on a first name basis with the nurses who tended to Mary around the clock. This particular morning around 5:30, one of our favorites was checking on Mary prior to shift change. I thought nothing of this until I heard her engaging in conversation with nonother than Mary herself!

I immediately stood up from my recliner, noticed the look of amazement on the nurse's face, while Mary continued to carry on the conversation. Once Mary noticed the nurse looking across the room, she turned towards me and excitedly exclaimed, "hey Mickey, I didn't know you were here! I was just discussing with the nurse that someone needs to tend to the special needs man at the nursing home. My spirit has been traveling to places around the world that I've always wanted to see. I know that I'm dying, and I don't know how much longer I have, but before I die, I just needed to tell someone to take care of the man with downs-syndrome!"

To say the least, I was speechless! I had often heard that sometimes when someone is approaching death, that the good Lord will give them a time of clarity to allow closure before they die. Honestly, at this very moment, I didn't know what to think other than God had answered our prayer and had healed her! Regardless of what had happened, I'll take it! While the nurse went to notify Mary's physician about her improved condition, I continued in conversation with Mary through tears of joy! At this point, Mary's sister had sat up in her recliner and asked, "is that Mary Ann talking?" Mary exclaimed, "yes, it is!" Mary's sister immediately got in on the excitement and joy of what had just happened. We all three started praising the Lord and decided it best not to contact those closest to us with the good news until later in the morning!

With this being Sunday morning after Thanksgiving, the physician who normally tended to Mary wouldn't be in until later in the day or possibly not until Monday. So, the physician who arrived to check on Mary was not as familiar with her case as her mostly regular physician. He promptly introduced himself while perusing Mary's medical records in a folder in which he was holding. He then asked Mary how she felt and she said I feel great! I then stated that, "we got our miracle doc! She's been miraculously healed!" He then asked me in an inquiring voice, "how's that? It's not wise to jump to any conclusions!" I then stated and asked, "based on her current condition, sitting up in bed and carrying on a normal conversation without any difficulty; and based on the brain scan that you're observing in your hand, is this the condition you'd expect to find this patient in?" He replied, "absolutely not! I would expect her to be catatonic as indicated in last night's report." I then replied emphatically, "exactly!" He then stated, "look, I'm not being negative, I just think it wise to conduct further testing before jumping to any conclusions." With him having said that, he requested a speech therapist to evaluate Mary along with a follow-up brain scan to be conducted the following day on Monday.

While I appreciated the professionalism displayed on the physician's behalf, I wasn't going to allow anything to hinder how relieved and excited I was about Mary's healing! At this time, we were notified that a speech therapist, once she finished at church, would be in to evaluate Mary around noon or so. Now, that we had somewhat of a plan going forward, we notified those closest to us about
Mary's improvement. Unfortunately, for those who had been visiting

from out of town, the majority had already traveled back home.

For those who lived locally, some would be visiting after church that morning with the remainder visiting after church that evening. While the news spread of the miracle that we had received, I went to get a bite to eat and had some much-needed alone time with the Lord along the way.

While I was rejoicing both outwardly and inwardly for what I had just witnessed, I still had this check in my spirit. I had a lot of questions running through my mind that I spoke out loud to the Lord (as if he needed me to). If it was brain cancer (which the Saturday physician believed), was the cancer throughout Mary's body removed as well? If not! Why not? Were all the blood clots forming within her body dissolved or removed? Was the area in her duodenum where the stent had been implanted fully functioning? Had she regained use of the left side of her body that was somewhat paralyzed due to the strokes? In the excitement of having Mary upright, clear minded, and conversational after knocking on heaven's door. Suddenly, I was over-whelmed by the swing of emotions from one extreme to the other! As is often the case, once I shut my trap and quiet my mind to hear from the Lord. He comforts me through His word in His timing. In this case, He does it again with one of my favorite verses, "Be still and know that I am God, I will be exalted among the nations, I will be exalted in the earth." (NIV, Psalms 46:10) In other words Mickey, stop trying to figure it out son and rest in Me!

The speech therapist arrived around 1230. When entering the room and laying eyes on an upright smiling Mary, she couldn't help but exclaim, "oh, my God." You see, she had evaluated Mary as NPO (nothing by mouth) for the last 4 consecutive days. To our amazement, once the evaluation was finished, the speech therapist declared, "she can have anything that she wants by mouth, with one exception. I want her to begin with nectar thickness fluids as opposed to water or regular thickness fluids. This is simply a precaution! I have never in my career removed a patient from NPO to no restrictions whatsoever in a matter of hours. So, I'm being a little cautious. You'd probably be fine drinking regular fluids, but I don't want to chance getting any fluid in your lungs. The nectar thickness fluids will prevent this from happening." We had our first medical confirmation that something supernatural had taken place!

Throughout the remainder of the day, it was a blessing to be able to interact with Mary in a way that I never thought possible again in this lifetime. But here we were, reminiscing about old times with family and friends as we had done at numerous gatherings many times before. As is often the case in what would be considered a somewhat social setting, I oftentimes find myself on the perimeter of the room observing as opposed to interacting. In this case, it allowed others to spend some time with Mary while I took a breather. I must admit that it lightened my heart to observe the expressions of hope, peace and joy on the faces of loved ones as opposed to the expressions of tears, sadness and grief from the previous day. Honestly, while this was a priceless moment that I will always be thankful for, I couldn't help but wonder how long it would last!

While still in deep thought, my son had entered the room and he inquired as to whether Mary's primary physician was aware of her improved condition. I told him that I didn't think that he was going to be in residence today. He stated that he had just passed him in the lobby and that he had his physician's jacket on. So, my son left to find Mary's physician to spread the good news. Within minutes, he returned with the good doctor in tow. Upon entering Mary's room, her physician (who is a mountain of a man), exclaimed, "Mrs. Mary Blakely, just look at you! Sitting upright in bed, smiling and talking your little head off! What happened?" Mary smilingly replied, "I reckon I decided to wake up, doc!" The room immediately erupted with laughter! He proceeded to sit on the edge of her bed and conduct some general observations. After reviewing her medical chart and jotting down some notes, he then stood up and began to leave the room.

Before exiting, while shaking his head in disbelief, he turned around and proclaimed, "I know that you folks are some praying people! All I know is that we didn't do anything medically to improve Mrs. Mary's condition. Yet, here she is, with new life breathed into her. What happened here is clearly above my pay grade!" I then followed him out into the hallway to inquire as to how this changed the game-plan. While still in disbelief, he responded, "it changes it tremendously! For starters, thankfully, they'll be no need for hospice tomorrow! We'll then run a series of scans and tests beginning tomorrow morning. The results will then dictate what course or courses of action to implement to advance Mrs. Mary's health. Having said that, all I know is that my brother needs some of what Mrs. Mary got." I assured him that his brother remained in our daily prayers as he headed towards the elevators.

While I was speaking with Mary's physician, our last visitors of the day had arrived. This group of friends were the last visitors from the previous night as well. The group which included our former pastor who anointed Mary with oil and prayed for her healing. As I entered Mary's room, I observed that this group had encircled her bed. Their faces displayed expressions of amazement as they observed and listened to Mary speak. It was at that moment, I realized Mary was literally preaching God's word about our salvation through Christ Jesus. How she had seen firsthand the gates of heaven and had conversation spirit to Spirit with God. She kept repeating, if you don't know Jesus as Saviour, you need to receive Him today because He is real! It was at that point our former pastor confessed that he came prepared to minister but God had already provided. This groups general consensus was, "we know what we saw last night and we know what we see tonight, God has truly provided!"

Now that everyone has left and Mary's sister was staying the night at our home, it was just Mary and I. What a difference a few hours in the Lord makes! It had only been approximately 17 hours since Mary sit up in bed and started having a conversation with her nurse. As I sat next to her and cupped her left hand, I noticed that she had regained some use in her left arm and hand. She then turned to face me. With eyes locked on one another, she smilingly stated, "wow! What a ride we've been on boy!" I replied, "you're telling me! From my perspective, it's been peaks and valleys, peaks and valleys continuously! I know that the Lord is teaching me to be content and praise Him in the valley just like I do during those mountaintop experiences, but it is hard!" She replied, "I can only imagine what you're going through. Despite my physical condition, I am pain free and have a peace that passes all understanding in the natural. I would much rather be in the bed than sitting in your chair. I would have probably left by now. I wouldn't trade places with you for nothing!" On that note, I assured her that she would be present just as I have been. We then thanked God for His goodness, said our prayers and kissed goodnight. I was very thankful that we were able to have this conversation!

Ironically, the first visitors the following morning were the two representatives from the local hospice facility. They had not been informed of Mary's improved condition so, they were pleasantly surprised when observing Mary sitting up in bed, smiling, and engaging in conversation. I replied, "I guess ya'll weren't notified of Mary's improvement. I'm so sorry that ya'll have made a wasted trip." They smiled and spoke in unison that there were other patients that unfortunately required their services that morning. So, this is not a wasted trip. We couldn't think of a better way to start the day than with a praise report with what the Lord has done in Mary's life. This is awesome! Before leaving, they reminded me about the contact information provided in case we needed their services at a later date. I thought to myself, I hope that's not anytime soon!

Immediately after the hospice reps had left, Mary's physician entered and proceeded to go over all the tests he had ordered for the day. He informed me that Mary would be out of room for the majority of the day. It would be wise for me to get away and remove myself as best as I could from the spousal responsibilities required while by her side. In agreeing with his advice, I prayed with Mary before kissing her goodbye and heading home. As was often the case while driving home during this season, my mind was all over the place. I began to entertain some of the same questions that had crossed my mind the previous day. Thankfully, before I got too far down any of these rabbit holes of thought, the Holy Spirit brought to my remembrance a scripture that has been so beneficial to me over the years! "Casting down imaginations, and every high thing that exalteth itself against the knowledge of God, bringing into captivity every thought to the obedience of Christ!" (2 Corinthians 10:5, KJV)

Once arriving home, I was greeted by the pleasant aroma of fresh brewed coffee which my sister-in-law had ready and waiting. During this journey, I believe that this was the only time that it was just the two of us at home. In the beginning, Mary would have been home as well but, ever since she had been hospitalized, her sister and I would rotate back and forth as needed. So, this gave my sister-in-law and me the opportunity to simultaneously catch our breath and share our thoughts. Of course, she immediately inquired as to whether I believed Mary was healed or not. I told her that there's definitely been some healing going on but, to what extent, I don't know. I then updated her on all the tests and evaluations that would be taking place today. I think it wise that we just be patient and wait for the results to have a better understanding as opposed to trying to figure things out like I had attempted to do earlier while driving home. This prompted both of us to laugh with her replying, "I know what you mean." It was a blessing to share some laughter at this time! "A merry heart doeth good like a medicine, but a broken spirit drieth the bones." (KJV, Proverbs 17:22)

After taking care of some things around the house, I retreated to the upper room (rec room) to watch some television. I don't remember how much television I watched; I just remember waking up several hours later. Evidently, my sister-in-law had retreated to her bedroom and slept as well. With both of us anticipating the results of Mary's scans, tests, and evaluations, we headed to the hospital after preparing a couple of coffees to go. As always, we drove separate vehicles to the hospital to ensure that we always had a mode of transportation when the other spent the night at home. As I drove closer and closer to the hospital, I imagined that my sister-in-law's mind was running rampant with thoughts as was mine. Upon arriving at the hospital, I immediately went inside while she stayed behind to call her husband.

As I entered Mary's room, she was sitting up in bed watching one of her favorite programs on HGTV. When making this observation, I immediately shook my head completing a double take of what I was witnessing. This was the first time during this hospital stay that Mary had been capable of what would be considered normal behavior for her. Once she noticed me, she immediately called out, "hey boy! How are you doing?" I responded, "I'm doing fine now that I see how well you're doing!" While taking my place at her side, we continued to chitchat about the day's activities with her concluding that she was wore out from all that had been required from her. I proceeded to ask her if any results from the various tests had been disclosed to her. She replied that she made it clear to her primary physician that she didn't want to go over any results until I was present. At that moment, as if on cue, Mary's primary physician entered her room to go over the results.

He proceeded to tell us that while there were some positive results to the point of head scratching, there were also some results that warrant a great deal of concern. I'll begin with the positive. The brain scan conducted came back crystal clear except for indicators from the two strokes you've previously incurred. There is no sign of cancer and/or hemorrhaging as indicated on the scan taken 3 days ago. This in itself is nothing short of miraculous, which by the way, caused me to scratch my head and smile. Of course, your speech evaluation conducted yesterday, which you passed with flying colors, falls into this category as well. Your occupational and physical evaluations also show signs of improvement. You're now capable of dismounting your bed and tending to personal needs with some assistance. Prior to yesterday, you were totally bedridden needing complete assistance. These improvements are simply amazing! Now for the areas of concern.

While I know that you all were believing that a total and complete physical healing had taken place, unfortunately, that simply is not the case. I wish it were! The duodenal cancer is still very much present and active in Mary's body. I must admit that this also has me scratching my head. Why wouldn't whatever/whoever removed and healed the brain cancer/hemorrhaging, also remove and heal this area as well! This doesn't make any sense to me! In agreement I replied, "that makes two of us!" However, Mary's physician continued, with the improvements in your physical body, we can now get back on track to continue your chemotherapy treatments sooner rather than later. To assist in improving your overall physicality, you will begin both occupational and physical therapy tomorrow morning. The goal is to have you promoted to the physical rehabilitation floor by weeks' end. In conclusion, he finished by stating that it's hard to believe that just 2 days ago I had called hospice care in.

As Mary's physician was exiting the room, her sister had just entered. I thought it best to give them some time together while I spoke with her physician out in the hallway. I proceeded to tell him that since Mary was experiencing no pain and required no medication for pain; I'm really caught off guard that the cancer is still prevalent in her body. Based on what the abdominal physician's assistant (Chapter 7, paragraph 1) had told me concerning Mary's level of pain at that time; I just assumed that since she wasn't in pain, that she had totally been healed of cancer! This has me both shaking and scratching my head! His response was somewhat unexpected but nonetheless very accurate. He stated, "Mr. Blakely, there's a lot of things concerning Mrs. Mary's condition that have me scratching my head! Despite all this, let's be thankful that now we're in a position to formulate and implement a treatment plan as opposed to managing her condition in hospice care!" I responded with a big, "Amen!"

The next 3 days were such a blessing! Mary was progressing through her respective therapies at a very rapid pace. The sparkle in her eye and the expression on her face indicated that she was determined to get healthy enough to resume chemotherapy and kick this cancer in the butt! Her sister and I provided the encouragement that she needed to press forward at the times she needed it most. We continued to thank God and give Him the glory, the honor and the praise that He so rightfully deserves! For me personally, this was the turning point that I needed to come face to face with in my relationship with God pertaining to this season. That Garden of Gethsemane moment! That moment where you must fully surrender your will to His wisdom and trust His unfailing love during the most difficult and heartbreaking of circumstances. That moment where like Jesus confessed before His betrayal, "Father, if You are willing, remove this cup from me; yet not my will, but Yours be done." (Luke 22:42, NASB)

With Mary's physicality improving by leaps and bounds over the past 3 days, I decided to go home for the night. Due to her progress, she would be assigned to the Rehab Floor the following day. This would require several mandatory items which would assist in her continued improvement throughout her stay during rehabilitation. So, my primary assignment at this point was to collect this list of items and show up bright and early the next morning. Once I had packed up the list of items, I called it a day and settled in for the night. As I lay in bed with mostly positive thoughts crossing my mind, I was excited with anticipation concerning Mary's upgrade to the Rehab Floor. Little did I know that while I was drifting off to sleep, a familiar circumstance during this journey was in the process of thwarting these plans!

Upon entering Mary's hospital room the following morning, it felt like I had walked into a morgue! I immediately noticed that Mary was in her bed which brought me great comfort. However, as I approached her bed, I realized that she had that catatonic stare on her face which to say the least was very concerning. As I stood there in disbelief, Mary's sister entered the room and softly spoke, "I'm so sorry sweetie! At approximately 1:00 A.M., Mary had another stroke. She's mostly been like this ever since. Since her condition was stable, I thought it best to let you get your rest as opposed to notifying you so early in the morning." I quietly responded, "you did the right thing!"

I then took my place by Mary's side, simultaneously caressing her hand while praying in the Spirit. Honestly, I was too distraught to think clearly about anything at that moment. It's simply heart wrenching to watch your soulmate endure all the sufferings she'd encountered on this journey. She'd worked so hard to get her physicality back to a place where treatment would resume in the near future. She was supposed to upgrade to the Rehab Floor today but, that plan had now been nixed. As I continued to grieve at Mary's side, her Neurologist gently got my attention to go over her brain scan. He pointed out the area that indicated where the most recent stroke had occurred. The good news was that it didn't appear to be as severe as the previous stroke was. However, instead of Mary being upgraded for advanced physical rehab as noted earlier; he had ordered occupational, physical and speech evaluations be conducted to determine the level of rehab required in each area. As if on cue, the therapists conducting the evaluations were front and center ready to do their thing!

While the evaluations were being conducted, my sister-in-law and I took time to notify family members and friends about Mary's unfortunate setback. Of course, the toughest calls for me to make were to our son and daughter. Our hopes had been lifted sky high since Mary's rapid improvement had taken place. Now, I find myself calling to inform them about their mother having another stroke. To say the least, despite our faith in God, the three of us were deflated because of this sudden turn of events. During the conversations, we encouraged one another as best as we could. By God's grace, Mary had worked her way back from this predicament once before so, we held fast that by His grace she could do it again!

The following day, which was Saturday December 2, 2017, believe it or not, Mary began the three phases of rehab which had been ordered. Overnight, some healing had manifested itself in her body to the point where she could begin therapy. Due to this blessed turning of events, Mary's sister headed back home out of state as she had planned prior to Mary taking a turn for the worse. Mary was no longer in a catatonic state of mind as she was the previous day. However, the effects of the stroke were noticeable, especially when she spoke and attempted to use her extremities on her left side. Nonetheless, she had this wry grin on her face and that glint in her eye that indicated it was game on!

Over the next 4 days, Mary worked her butt off to improve her overall physicality to be promoted to the Rehab Floor. I don't want to paint a picture in your mind here of Mary up walking and doing things unassisted, because that would be far from the truth.

However, she improved from being totally bedridden again to a place where she could do these things with assistance. You're required to be at a certain level physically and mentally during therapy on the Rehab Floor. The Rehab Floor is no joke! It will require everything that Mary has within her spiritually and mentally for her to endure what will be physically expected of her. I can't literally put into words how proud I am of my wife at this moment of being promoted. She's literally fighting for her life with everything she has!

CHAPTER ELEVEN
REHAB FLOOR

Mary has finally been promoted to the Rehab Floor! It's taken 3 weeks for her to accomplish this goal! Honestly, it's only by God's amazing grace that she has endured her journey to this point. The first day was mainly a time of orientation to get acquainted with the staff and scheduling of therapies taking place each day. There is no medical treatment provided per se on the Rehab Floor, strictly rehabilitation. However, due to Mary's abdominal impairment, a waiver was granted for the continued use of TPN (nutrition by IV) to supplement her meals as to receive proper nourishment. At this point in time, she had an increase in appetite which thankfully, led to her eating more than she had since beginning this journey. Despite Mary's condition, there were a lot of reasons to remain hopeful!

Once we had finished with the orientation process, I had a big surprise for Mary. Knowing in advance how challenging rehabilitation would be for her; I knew that she would need all the encouragement and motivation that could be mustered up! She loved looking at pictures, especially pictures of family! So, I had developed pictures from our family photo shoot in late October and assembled a photo album. I also had a 2 x 3-foot canvas picture of our entire family made to hang on our living room wall at home.

This picture has been hanging at home for the past 2 weeks in anticipation of Mary's arrival. Since this hasn't happened, I thought what a surprise it would be for her to enter her rehab room with this picture being the first thing that she sees. It worked to perfection! Her face lit up like a Christmas tree!

That first night together in rehab is one that I will always hold dear to my heart! As noted earlier, there is no medical care per se, so there are no bells and whistles going off at all hours of the day. Also, the room is more like one you would find at a hotel as opposed to a hospital. The furnishings were somewhat high-end and very accommodating. With our family portrait hanging on the wall, Mary and I sat side by side watching TV as if we were in the privacy of our own home. I suppose in our minds we were. I found myself hoping that there would be many more nights like this to come. Only time would tell!

Before calling it a night, Mary and I reflected over the past 35 years of our life together. We both agreed that we had been blessed beyond measure of what we could have hoped for or dreamed of! Despite the valley years that we had and currently are experiencing in our life, God has always provided! Not always in the way that we had drawn up in our minds but, in the way that was most beneficial to us according to His purpose and plans for our lives (Romans 8:28)! We both realized simultaneously that our faith had been increased during these past experiences to assist in preparing us for the amount of faith that would be required to endure this current circumstance. We thanked God for His goodness as the two of us fell asleep.

Upon awakening the next morning, I was ushered out fairly quickly as no visitors are allowed to be present during rehabilitation hours. The staff requires the full devotion and attention of the patient and visitors were considered to be a distraction. As I was driving to our home, I was engaged in quite a lively conversation with my Heavenly Father. In this particular case, I was the one doing the majority of the talking. As I was driving down the road speaking about all kinds of different scenarios allowing myself to get whipped up into a frenzy.

Suddenly, the Holy Spirit shouted just stop! I replied with I did! I stopped at the redlight Lord. He responded with I'm not talking about the redlight. I'm talking about you wasting a lot of your time and energy allowing your imagination to run wild at this time. You need to stop this. I know what you're going through and while I love you beyond measure, unfortunately, like most of my children, you are your own worst enemy at times. It pains me to see you struggle with these self-inflicted wounds especially at a time when you're already hurting due to Mary's condition.

I know you trust me, Mickey! So, as you continue to cast this care upon me, learn to leave it with me. I know that you are tired and laboring during this season. Most of my children struggle during a similar circumstance as yours. It's because you attempt to persevere through the circumstance on your own. At times, you allow me to help carry the load. During these times, you are sound minded and stable in your ways. That's why you find yourself trapped in a vicious cycle of rollercoaster emotions when you attempt to be self-sustaining. You need to choose to stay yoked up with me continually. As you continue to learn of me, you'll mature spiritually. Which in turn, you'll allow me to do the heavy lifting! This is My plan for you during this season. If God is not a God of love, why would He chastise us when we most need it! (Proverbs, 3:12)

Once being recentered spiritually, I continued home to check on a few things before returning to spend time with Mary. She had had a very promising first day of rehabilitation by accomplishing the daily goals established by her team. Having said this, when I asked Mary how her day went, she replied, "it hurt like hell! I'm not in any hurting pain or anything but it required a lot of energy and
I'm really tired and sore." Immediately, I realized just how tough rehab was on her based on the use of the "h" word. This was way out of character for her! I then comforted her as best as I could before we settled in for another night.

Mary started her 4th day of rehab today which also happens to be December 9th, my father's 82nd birthday. I'm hoping that Mary's sister will return from out of town in time for me to visit and celebrate this occasion. I can't help but think that if this happens, it'll be the first time in 36 years that Mary will not be at my side for my father's birthday. Meanwhile, I'm to shadow Mary's rehab team today for training purposes. The goal is for Mary to be fully rehabbed in 3 weeks, discharged back home and continue chemotherapy. At that time, while the necessary equipment will be provided, I must have an understanding as to what to expect concerning her in home care. Honestly, while observing what is required of Mary physically during rehab, no wonder it hurt like "h"! I don't think I could endure what's required of her!

Thankfully, Mary's sister did return in time for me to visit with my parents and celebrate my father's birthday. It's about a 2 hour round trip drive from the hospital to my parents' home. It seems that while driving alone is when my imagination attempts to get the better of me during this season. To combat this, I've started to listen to Christian music more often than not to help keep my mind occupied. I really needed this on this particular trip due to the emotions involved with Mary being absent. However, just like the previous two visits to my parents during this season, once my momma answered the door, I was a hot mess once again!

I know I'm biased, but my father is a most remarkable man for many reasons. Most importantly, he enthusiastically has a great compassion for people akin to our Lord & Savior Jesus! Especially the less fortunate and the so-called underdogs in society. This is an area in which he and Mary share a kindred spirit. An area in which they didn't share a kindred spirit (due to no fault of their own), my father could eat all the sweets and desserts in sight without gaining an ounce, while Mary (like most of us) could gain weight just by looking at it. So, during holiday season, daddy loved to pick on Mary concerning the sweets and desserts issue while simultaneously conjuring up a plan to be a blessing to those that the Lord impressed upon their hearts. Sadly, the thing I remember most about this visit is the emptiness I saw within my father due to the absence of his partner in crime during this holiday season.

As I was driving back to the hospital, I needed to talk to the Lord in a bad way! The emptiness that I had observed within my father is exactly the way that I felt. Despite my faith in God's word, I continued to have this troubling in my heart, this spiritual intuition if you will, this knowingness in my spirit that Mary wasn't going to survive this. The difference being this time is that my heart has been prepared and is fully invested to finally accept God's will for both our lives. I'm tired of being tossed to and fro by this circumstance!

So, by God's amazing grace, I have humbled myself and chosen to receive a wonderful measure of His peace that passes understanding. I have learned to be content with Mary's condition and am ready to do all things required of me through Christ who strengthens me! (Philippians 4:11,13 KJV)

While driving and praising God for this breakthrough moment, my sister-in-law called and informed me that she had ordered steaks for the three of us to eat from Longhorn's Steakhouse. That she had already paid the tab and all I had to do was pick them up. Sounded good to me! After arriving at Mary's room, we blessed the food and began to chit chat while we were eating.

Fascinated by Mary's appetite, I couldn't help but comment, "wow! What brought this on?" Mary responded, "I asked the staff if I could eat steak and they said I could if it was a very tender filet, so there you go!" She ate approximately half of her meal before pushing it away then stated that she wanted to go to sleep now. We said our prayers and I thanked my sister-in-law for all she was doing before I headed home. With Mary's sister being there, I felt comfortable going home and sleeping in my own bed for a change.

As I lay in bed that night, I had all kinds of thoughts and scenarios racing through my mind. While choosing to entertain some of these possible scenarios (even the bad ones), I continued to have that peace that passes all understanding as opposed to being tossed about mentally and emotionally as I had experienced previously during these moments. At this moment, that still, small voice that resides within reminded me to cast these concerns upon the Lord to allow Him to carry the load. And when you do, make sure that you leave them there as well. By God's grace, I was able to be obedient to this encouragement! Next thing I remember is waking up 8 hours later. I was thankful for the reminder that obedience to God always brings blessings. (KJV, Deuteronomy 28:1-2)

As I returned and entered the hospital, I was immediately greeted by Mary's sister in the lobby. She had this look of concern written all over her face, which honestly, is to be expected considering the circumstances. I, of course, asked her what's going on? She said that she thought that Mary had given up. I countered with, I don't believe that she's given up! I think that this rehab program is really demanding and that she's worn out! If she doesn't want to rehab any longer, she can just say the word and put a stop to it at any time. She replied with, maybe so! She just looks really tired and like you said just worn out. I chuckled and said, watch what the therapists put her through today. In the end, you'll be declaring just like I did that you couldn't do what they require of her. After watching Mary's physical therapy for about 15 minutes, her sister declared, "oh my God!" How is she doing that? I couldn't!"

With it being Sunday, Mary's therapy sessions were cut short to half a day. Once she had settled down and rested, I heated up her leftover steak which she promptly finished off. After eating, her sister and I questioned Mary as to whether she wanted to continue with the rehab program. She stated that even though it hurt like "h" (not hell this time), that as long as she was able to participate, she would do so. Even though her voice was somewhat shaky and unsettled, I could still see that fire and determination in her steely blue eyes!

That evening, Mary's sister stayed at our home while I stayed the night with Mary. Again, we shared a wonderful evening watching tv as if we were in the confines of our home. The difference being from our first night together here was that Mary was elevated in her hospital bed as opposed to sitting by my side. It didn't really matter, as long as we were at each other's side holding hands. At this point, some of our friends had brought over a Christmas tree along with other decorations for Mary's room. As we continued to watch tv in the midst of dancing Christmas lights, we both drifted off to sleep until the following morning.

Immediately the following morning, I was ushered out as to not interfere with Mary's full day of scheduled therapy. However, before leaving, we prayed for Mary to continue to receive strength and healing to endure what is expected of her today. By this point, Mary's primary daytime nurse had been joining in for daily prayer whenever her scheduled permitted. It always brought me great comfort knowing that Mary was left in more than capable hands whenever I left the facility. As I drove home this time, there was no chastisement or conversation with God per se. I just praised Him with everything that I am while listening to Christian music!

Once arriving home, my sister-in-law (as usual when she's here) already had a pot of coffee brewed. As we sipped our coffee, we reflected on the past couple of months and how Mary had survived brain cancer and 3 strokes. We knew that it was only due to God's will for Mary's life that she was currently able to continue to fight for her life as we speak. She asked me point blank if I was prepared and had a plan for if and when Mary returns home. I informed her that I had been in constant contact with the hospital's social worker and that I was properly trained and prepared. She told me she was just checking in case there was anything that she could do to be of assistance. I told her not that I'm aware of, that her presence alone was sufficient for the time being.

Upon returning to Mary's room, as soon as I gazed into her eyes, I could tell that something was wrong. Those steely blue eyes which previously displayed fire and determination were missing. Instead, I found myself gazing into a pair of saddened and somewhat defeated eyes. As if someone had extinguished the fire that had flamed within. I then gently leaned over and whispered to her, "what's wrong baby?" She proceeded to tell me that her legs hurt so bad that she was unable to complete most of her therapy today. That even though the therapists were encouraging and informed her that everyone has an off day, she believed that something was wrong. She further stated that the therapists relayed this information up the chain of command. That when Mary's doctor made his nightly rounds, hopefully we would have a better understanding.

Shortly after we had eaten supper, Mary's doctor made his nightly visit. I could tell by the serious expression on his face that there was cause for concern. Once he had given Mary a thorough looking over, he motioned for me to follow him to the hallway. This would be my first and only interaction with this particular doctor. While he was very professional, he conveyed the areas of concern to me in a compassionate manner. He stated that he had ordered a series of scans to be conducted over the next couple of days.

That during this time as well, Mary's therapy would continue for her upper body, but her lower body therapy would be suspended pending the results of the scans. The most alarming topic of discussion was he needed to know if Mary had a DNR (do not resuscitate) order in place. I informed him that her living will was on file which stated she didn't want to be revived if she expired here. He gently nodded and patted me on the back before departing to his next patient.

The next couple of days consisted of Mary working in upper body therapy between the series of scans that had been ordered. On the last of these days, our daughter and granddaughter were allowed to visit during the early afternoon hours. It worked out perfectly for our daughter to do Mary's nails while I entertained our granddaughter. As our daughter was finishing her momma's nails, Mary's nurse came in and told the therapist in waiting that all therapy for Mary had been suspended due to multiple blood clots found in her legs. While this news was certainly disturbing, Mary shouted, "thank God!" This proclamation prompted everyone present to somewhat laugh with a hint of concern.

That evening after everyone had left, Mary and I found ourselves in conversation pertaining to the current circumstance. The primary concern conveyed by her team was that continued therapy could result in a blood clot or clots breaking free causing another stroke. It was best to err on the side of caution at this point. We were advised that all hands were on deck reviewing Mary's case to determine the

best course of action from this point forward. They were hoping to have a plan of action in place by the following afternoon. After watching a little tv, we prayed for guidance and wisdom for all parties involved with this process. We also thanked God for measuring out the manifestation of His healing power to Mary's body according to His plan and purposes for her life.
(Proverbs 19:21, NIV)

Thankfully, after an unsettled night of attempting to sleep, I could remain at Mary's side due to her therapy being suspended. For this reason as well, we were allowed to sleep in. Not realizing the lateness of the morning hour (approaching noon), suddenly, a dear friend of mine dropped in to take me out for lunch and to give me a much-needed break. We've known each other for 30 plus years through both church and work. He's one of my inner circle friends that has always been there for me throughout the years when most needed. This would be one of those most needed times. He and I said our goodbyes to Mary and her sister as we headed to a local restaurant.

While eating, I caught him up on Mary's current condition. That we were pretty much at a standstill until her medical team determined what to do next. We're actually hoping to hear something this afternoon. He then changed the content of the conversation to assist in mentally giving me a break. We frequented a lot of concerts together throughout the years which became our main topic of conversation from this point forward. After we had reminisced about past concerts and while talking about upcoming events, I received a phone call from my sister-in-law. She informed me that Mary's team, including her three main doctors, were waiting in private to speak to me. I remember taking a deep breath before informing my friend that I needed to return to the hospital immediately.

Upon returning to the hospital, my sister-in-law was waiting in the lobby to lead me to the meeting room. Once entering, I recognized the heads and/or their assistants of the departments of the main hospital, Neurology, Oncology and Rehabilitation Therapy. I could discern by the expression on the Oncology reps' face that this was not going to result in a good report. She, Mary and I had developed a pleasant acquaintanceship throughout this journey. It didn't hurt that she had the same first name as our daughter's. The summation of the report concluded that the cancer had spread to Mary's lungs and was terminal. Due to this diagnosis, all department heads indicated that no further treatment could be provided. They unanimously recommended Hospice care!

As my sister-in-law burst into tears while collapsing in her chair, I just stood there emotionless for a moment until the Oncology rep approached to comfort me when I then burst into tears. I told her that I was hoping that this moment would never occur, but, now that it has, I need to notify the kids and at some point, have a talk with Mary. The Oncology rep then stated to me that while no one has notified Mary of this diagnosis, she probably already knows in her heart and won't be as caught off guard as you might think. On that note, I excused myself and went to notify my children about their mother's diagnosis.

I don't believe that there's anything in life that can even partially prepare you for moments such as this. That's why in this moment, I'm just pacing around one wing of the hospital praying in the Spirit until I feel led by the Holy Spirit to call our children. When that moment comes, I call our son first, he's the oldest. Our son is a man of very few words especially on the phone. Even though he's a tender-hearted man, he typically doesn't display a lot of emotion like his old man. He's more like Mary in this regard. I would probably be considered a cry baby by most people's standards. That's fine by me, it's who I am. Our conversation goes pretty much like I expected, brief and to the point. While I do hear some cracking in his voice once he receives the news, he informs me that he hates to hear this and that he'll stop by the hospital after work. Now, to call our daughter.

Our daughter is a cross between Mary and me. While she's capable of displaying emotion, it's typically not to the extent that I do. She also doesn't have any problem conversing or asking questions with anyone whether on the phone or in person. I expected this call to be a longer and more in-depth phone conversation. I wasn't disappointed.

Our daughter's voice resonated with the amount of emotion that I had anticipated. Once the initial shock of the conversation had somewhat subsided, she started asking the questions that crossed her mind. I answered to the best of my ability ending with the answer to her final question, "what happens now?" I replied with, "we meet with Hospice rep's tomorrow morning to decide that." In conclusion, despite the circumstance, I was very thankful for the conversations that I had with both our children. I needed that constant part of my life more than ever considering a big part of my life had just been turned upside down!

During Mary's tenure at the hospital (which now has reached 1 month), it seems that 2 a.m. is when we would have our deepest conversations. At 2 a.m. on December 15, 2017, this fact would continue to hold water. It is at this moment when I feel led to engage in the hardest conversation that I have ever had in my life. The moment in which I tell Mary about the catastrophic diagnosis. As I was gently caressing her left hand, she smilingly turned towards me as we quietly exchanged "hey baby's." I then proceeded to tell her that we needed to have a serious talk. She responded with, "how much time do I have?" I thought to myself, "wow! The Oncology rep was correct in her assumption!"

I continued by answering Mary's question, "baby, nobody knows how much time you have except for the good Lord." She then asked, "has the cancer spread to my brain again?" I responded with, "unfortunately, it has spread to your lungs." She chuckled and stated, "man! I didn't see that coming. Of all the ways I had imagined dying, I never suspected lung cancer. The only time I ever smoked was maybe a half a pack of Virginia Slims back in the day, you know, because women had come a long way baby" as she rolled her eyes. At this point she had me cracking up despite the circumstance. I just shook my head and commented, "you are something else! I was so dreading this conversation and yet we're sitting here cutting up and laughing. I just love you Mary Blakely, especially for making my life easier during life's toughest moments!"

As our conversation continued, she wanted to know what the gameplan was. I told her that we would be meeting with Hospice reps later today to decide. Basically, we have two options. We can go back home and have Hospice come in there, or we can be inresidence at a Hospice facility in either Nashville or Murfreesboro. She then asked me which route was I thinking. I told her I was thinking the in-residence option in Murfreesboro would be best for our family. However, I want to do what you're most comfortable with. If you want to go back home, then we'll go back home. She said that as long as you're able to be there with me, it doesn't matter to me. With that decision made, we both thanked God for His goodness and for His peace that passes understanding during this most trying of times. Surprisingly, we both slept very well the rest of the morning.

When meeting with the Hospice reps, the atmosphere was very pleasant. It's hard to believe that it had only been 3 weeks ago that we met due to Mary's brain cancer diagnosis. It felt like three years! Due to the familiarity developed from that meeting, we were able to get down to business rather quickly. With our decision having been made to reside at the Murfreesboro facility, we were informed that they wouldn't have a vacancy until the following day. With that information, the Rehab facility manager was able to make arrangements for Mary to stay put until that time. However, much later that evening, the night manager would have a difference of opinion!

With Mary being discharged to Hospice care the following day, I began to pack up all personal items and Christmas ornaments that we had accumulated over the past 9 days. What began as a promising step in Mary's rehabilitation to health, has suddenly become what I had most feared. That the cancer had spread before treatment could resume! While I was loading up our SUV, I found myself mentally mulling over what to do next. Should I take all this stuff home and get it over with or just leave it be for the time being. I have a tendency to just go ahead and complete tasks immediately at times, as opposed to thinking them through. I began speaking to the Spirit that resides within as to what should I do next. He immediately impressed upon me to go spend time with your wife. So, as I was walking back to Mary's room, He further impressed that you're simply transferring these items to Mary's Hospice room. There's no need for all the additional unloading and loading. In that moment, I realized how much my thinking had been skewed during this journey. How hard it had become to think clearly even while attempting simple tasks. Normally, this would have been a no-brainer. Thank God for His amazing grace! "My grace is sufficient for you, for my power is made perfect in your weakness" (2 Corinthians 12:9 KJV)

Once returning to Mary's room (or was it), Mary, her sister and I ate some supper and eventually attempted to settle in for the night around 11 p.m. It was at this time the night shift nurse informed us that the night manager had requested Mary be relocated to the hospital side. His reasoning was that since Mary was no longer rehabbing, she needed to be moved due to the fact that a new patient would be moving in. Even though this was true, the new patient wouldn't be moving in until Monday morning. That's why the day manager had arranged in the system for Mary to stay put. Despite this, he was adamant and determined that Mary was not going to stay another night in that room!

With his decision made, this sent the hospital side into a frenzy attempting to accommodate Mary literally at the midnight hour! As I'm writing this, I'm literally laughing out loud and shaking my head at the comedy of errors that ensued due to this decision. Let's just say that after 2-3 hours of events too numerous to mention, we found ourselves back in the same hospital room that Mary had spent almost a month in. Despite all the chaos, this actually turned out to be a blessing in disguise! Mary was reunited with who I would consider to be her favorite nurse. Yep, the nurse whom Mary was speaking with when she was healed of brain cancer.

While I both never met the night manager and disagreed with his decision, I was reminded of a valuable life lesson that early morning hour. Life is the most precious commodity that each of us possess. The kicker is, none of us actually know how much life we have left on this Earth. So, don't sweat the small stuff! The reality is that most of the things that confront us in life should be considered small stuff. We need to reconnect with that intrinsic childlike nature that God created each one of us with! Sure, some things in life merit serious concern and attention. Considering this, it is my deepest desire each morning to commune with my Heavenly Father to get my daily marching orders. To address what needs to be addressed, and to enjoy every moment of life to the fullest from that point forward. This is how Mary's time at the hospital concluded. With us laughing out loud and shaking our heads despite her failing condition. As I'm driving towards Murfreesboro to fill out paperwork, I find myself praying that this same positive mindset will carry forward. Ready or not, it's Hospice time!

CHAPTER TWELVE
LIFE AT HOSPICE

Upon arriving at the Hospice facility, I was met by my sister-in-law who felt led to be there for support. We left Mary in good hands at the hospital with my son's family and one of Mary's brothers until transportation arrived. The memory that I'll always cherish when departing Mary's hospital room that day, was our 16-month-old grandson standing by the bed and holding his Nona's hand. Mary loved being a grandmother! She often told me throughout this journey her one regret (if she didn't survive this), would be not having the opportunity to watch our grandchildren grow up. While I continued to enjoy that moment in my mind, I was suddenly brought back to the here and now by Hospice staff. It was time to fill out the necessary paperwork and proceed with the gameplan.

I would have to say that filling out paperwork with assistance from Hospice staff was one of the most humbling experiences in my life. It really put our circumstance in perspective! Mary's condition had deteriorated to the point where all that could be done was to manage her pain. However, according to Mary, by God's grace she felt no pain! Regardless, Hospice staff comforted me by reminding me that their job was to tend to Mary's needs while my job was to cast off the caregiver role and simply be her husband. While no one knows the number of days Mary has remaining except for the Lord (Job 14:5 Good News Translation), we want you and your family to enjoy your time together here as much as possible.

Once the legalities were out of the way, I began unloading our personal belongings and Christmas decorations into Mary's room.
We were informed that Mary wouldn't be here for another hour or so. Due to this, I decided to go bring us back something to eat from Chik-Fil-A while my sister-in-law arranged the room. With this being a Saturday night just 9 days before Christmas, you could imagine how busy Chik-Fil-A was. There was bumper to bumper double lines at the drive through with 4 employees outside, 2 managing each line. As I inched forward in line, I bumped the rear end of a pick-up truck. This initiated what I refer to as the ChikFil-A incident!

As soon as I bumped into the truck in front of me, one of the employees simultaneously approached my SUV to take my order. With my window down and my eyes full of tears (from thinking about Mary being in Hospice care), I surprisingly was capable to give her my order prior to dismounting my SUV to confront the man standing outside his truck. I thought, "oh Lord! I don't need this right now!" As I approached this fellow expecting the worst, he immediately defused the situation by commenting, "hey buddy, I hope your vehicle's okay? I have an extended, heavy-duty trailer hitch, so I'm good! There's no need to cry about it!" Relieved, I immediately shook his hand and responded, "thank you so much and God bless you! My wife Mary has just been put into Hospice care. That's why I'm crying." He responded with, "God bless you sir! I hope you have a Merry Christmas if that's possible. We'll be praying for your wife Mary!"

Now, back in my SUV waiting for the line to move forward, I find myself praising and thanking God for what potentially could have been a hassle but instead, turned into a blessing with even more people praying for my Mary. While still waiting in line, the employee who took my order approached and tapped on my window. In a very pleasant tone of voice, she stated, "sir, I overheard part of your conversation and I'm so sorry about your wife Mary. My church family and I will be praying for ya'll!" I smilingly commented, "thank you and God bless you and yours! I hope ya'll have a Merry Christmas!" As I continued to wait in line, I reflected on how it seems at times, the enemy works overtime during Christmas season to bum us out. Especially if things aren't going well in life! With Mary now being in Hospice care, this would certainly qualify as one of those times. At that moment, I had reached the window to pay for and receive my order. Before I could hand them my debit card, the young man handed me my order with a smile responding, "there's no charge sir! It's on the house! We're praying for you and your wife Mary. Hope you can have a Merry Christmas!" I was so overwhelmed with emotion that I couldn't muster up a response.

As I was working my way back through traffic to the Hospice facility, I was still overwhelmed emotionally by the goodness of God in that moment! You can say what you want to good or bad about church or the body of Christ whether you're a believer in Jesus or not. I've been at times as critical about the body of Christ as anybody I know. Sometimes I wonder if we have forgotten that we're supposed to be about our Heavenly Father's business as His only begotten Son, Jesus our Saviour was! The fact of the matter is, the body of Christ is comprised of human beings. Us humans, don't always get it right! At times, we get off track and follow our own agendas. It's because, well, pun intended, we're humans! The more important fact of the matter is that God is the same! Today, yesterday and forever! (Hebrews 13:8 KJV) So, despite the shortcomings of the body of Christ, it doesn't change who God is, who God's been, and who God will be for all eternity. So, at this moment! I'm thankful for the goodness and compassion of God displayed to me through 3 of his created human vessels!!! (Galatians 6:10 & Psalm 145:8-9 KJV)

Once arriving back at the hospice facility, my sister-in-law notified me that Mary had arrived and they were in the process of getting her settled in the room. This worked out perfectly as the two of us were able to eat in the break area while this was taking place. While eating, my sister- in-law noticed that I had been crying. Out of concern, she inquired as to what was going on. I shared with her about just being overwhelmed with emotion due to Mary now being in Hospice care which led us to the Chik-Fil-A incident.

After explaining that scenario to her, we found ourselves enjoying some much-needed laughter followed by tears of joy. Now it's time to reconnect with my wife!

The in-residence Hospice accommodations were (pun intended) so accommodating! Of course, the most precious object in the room was the one sitting up comfortably in bed. My wife Mary! While the Hospice staff finished settling her in, the Holy Spirit brought to my remembrance an article that I had read years ago about how the components of the human body were worth approximately $1.98 in value. Isn't it amazing, how the God of the universe can breathe the breath of life into less than 2 bucks worth of components, thus bringing into existence His crown of creation. In turn, if you're fortunate, one of His created beings may become your most treasured and precious companion throughout your life's journey. In this moment, I can't help but wonder how much life my precious Mary has left in her created human body before her spirit enters eternity and, in time, her remains return to the very components prior to her Creator breathing them into life. Life is so very precious! We need to enjoy it to the fullest!

Once at Mary's side, we embraced and the two of us were immediately overwhelmed by our emotions. Although we had both hoped that this journey would never reach this point, we knew deep in our hearts that it was a possibility. Despite this, we were determined to enjoy the time that we had left together. To properly kick this off, I proceeded to tell her about the Chik-Fil-A incident. This prompted us to laugh, cry and praise God for His goodness and kindness during this season. We finished off the evening by continuously holding hands while watching some tv. After the Hospice staff had tended to Mary that evening, they gently reminded me to get some much-needed sleep. Before dozing off, I thanked God that He had answered my prayer request from earlier while driving to Murfreesboro. That by His grace, that same positive mindset had been carried forward, despite the circumstance!

Once awakening after an awesome night's rest, I immediately rolled over and was greeted by a bright-eyed smiling Mary! We both simultaneously shouted, "what an awesome night's rest, right!" This was followed by a few seconds of joyous laughter. It's amazing that she still is experiencing no pain! This is such a blessing! There would be several visitors coming by today and they would get to see Mary pretty much being herself with the exception of her being confined to a bed. Part of me wanted to be selfish, keeping her all to myself! However, throughout this journey, I have realized that you need some alone time with the Lord to recharge your spiritual batteries. So, visitation allows you to accomplish this while others spend some quality time with Mary. Hospice care by definition in most cases is a type of health care that focuses on the palliation of a terminally ill patient's pain and symptoms while attending to their emotional and spiritual needs at the end of life. Hospice care prioritizes comfort and quality of life by reducing pain and suffering. The facility is also set up to accommodate family members of the terminally ill as well. They provide a nice break area with an assortment of beverages while you watch tv, a quiet place for prayer and meditation, plus big family rooms to congregate. Most of the time I would find myself in the break area still trying to wrap my head around what's taking place. Occasionally, you would find yourself joined by staff who has or someone who is currently experiencing the same circumstance as you are.

It never ceases to amaze me how we as humans can at times be so compassionate and considerate of one another despite our differences. Especially during times of tragedy. My encounters with others were very frequent during Mary's stay at Hospice. It's as if when life is hanging in the balance, life's playing field is balanced out. It really doesn't matter what one another's story is at this point. What matters most is that you recognize one another's pain and fear of losing a loved one to death. This, in my opinion prompts that goodness of God that resides within to well up and provide whatever is necessary to accommodate a fellow human being in need. Whether it be a gentle embrace for reassurance, a kind word or prayer for encouragement, or to share a meal while reminiscing about one another's loved ones for enjoyment. What a wonderful world it would be if this was our mindset continually throughout life!

One particular encounter that I feel led to share was one with a staff member. It was known throughout Mary's stay at Hospice that she really was going to miss not being a part of our grandchildren's lives. At this point, they were 16 & 9 months old respectively. While it was obvious that they knew who Nona was, Mary wanted to stick around for a few more years to carry on conversations with them. This bothered me as well. I would often voice my opinion to the Lord how unfair it was that Mary was being cheated out of this blessing. Evidently, I was thinking this out loud one day, which prompted this certain staff member to share the following story with me.

She, along with all the other staff members have a calling or a gifting if you will to provide whatever is required to help comfort all parties involved while your loved one translates from the natural to the spiritual realm. During this particular conversation, this staff member felt led to share her experience concerning her mother's passing and her not having the opportunity to spend time with her future granddaughter. She proceeded to tell me that her mother had died in a car accident when her mother was in her 30's. She had passed prior to her granddaughter ever being born. Nonetheless, one day, the nurse heard her daughter in her bedroom playing and she asked her then 4-year-old daughter who she was playing with. Her daughter responded, "I'm playing with my grandma." Puzzled, due to having never shown her daughter a picture of her grandmother, she dug a picture of her mother out of a drawer.

When showing the picture to her daughter, she responded, "yes, that's my grandma that I play with, but she left when you came in." After hearing this testimony, I became very emotional. She ended the conversation by stating, "it has been my experience throughout my life and time as a Hospice employee, that nothing is above God's pay grade. He truly works in ways that we are incapable of understanding. I believe with all my heart that Miss Mary will be spending plenty of time with her current and future grandchildren." "For my thoughts are not your thoughts, neither are your ways my ways, declares the Lord. For as the heavens are higher than the earth, so are my ways higher than your ways and my thoughts than your thoughts." (Isaiah 55:8-9 ESV)

Once this conversation had concluded, the Hospice nurse asked, "if there's anything that you need just let us know." Somewhat joking, I immediately responded, "as a matter of fact there is! I've got several Christmas presents that need to be wrapped." Without hesitation, she led me to a fellow staff member who could assist me with that. Within a couple of hours, not only were all the gifts wrapped and neatly placed around the Christmas tree in one of the family rooms; we put together a plan for our family to celebrate Christmas in that same family room around noon on Christmas Day. Staff would simply bring Mary into this room where we all could open gifts and watch "It's A Wonderful Life" (a family tradition) as we would at home. Staff along with volunteers would also be providing lunch for the entire facility that day as well. In that moment, I could envision our family celebrating Christmas as we always had!

As previously stated, no one knows the number of days that Mary has left to live or how many any of us have for that matter. However, there are signs both seen and unseen when a body begins to shut down. One of the physical signs is called mottling. Mottling is the blotchy, red-purplish marbling of the skin. It most frequently occurs first on the feet, then travels up the legs. Mottling is caused by the heart no longer being able to effectively pump blood throughout the body. Mottling typically appears during the last week of an individual's life. Mottling began to appear in Mary's feet after about 4-5 days in the Hospice facility. This was somewhat sooner than we had anticipated. At this same time, blood began to pool on the right-side of her face. Due to this, the entire right-side of her face was a deep purplish color.

It was at this point that we decided to limit visitation to only family members. These physical signs indicate that Mary will more than likely transition to the spiritual realm within the next week. My heart is as heavy as it's ever been!

Since Mary has entered this "mottling phase", the atmosphere in her room has changed dramatically! Prior to this, she was able to carry on normal conversations and interactions with people, watch television, and eat soft ice (one of her favorite things to do). Now, there is little conversation, no television watching, and no consumption of ice. When conscious, she spends most of the time staring at 2 different locations on the ceiling. We were briefed ahead of time that this type of behavior is typical during this "phase". That as her body begins to shut down, she will be able to see into the spiritual realm. I noticed at these times, the expression upon her face was that of amazement! When asked what she saw, she responded, "I see Jesus!" This happened twice that I'm aware of. Once when her sister asked her, and again when I asked her.

I don't know if I can put into words exactly what I'm experiencing during this "phase", but I'll try. While I've had my Garden of Gethsemane moment, where I relinquished my will and accepted for God's will to be done. I feel this deeper pulling or tearing away from my soul if you will. It must be as Mary's body is shutting down, her very soul is beginning to ungraft from mine. I believe with all my heart that when we were married over 35 years ago, our souls were bound together in the name of Jesus. Over the years, our souls were intertwined to the point where we became as one. This ungrafting is causing pain unlike any that I've ever experienced in my life. It's a deep, guttural pain of loss which leaves me feeling helpless and empty inside. The feeling of I wish I could prevent Mary from dying but I can't. I don't like it!!!

Over the next couple of days, I spent as much time as possible at Mary's side. While she was sleeping, I would simply hold and caress her hand as I reminisced about our life together. What a wonderful life it had been! We had our challenges at times; however, we chose to stick it out and to remain together through thick and thin. Some of our friends would occasionally comment that Mary and I made marriage look easy. I believe there's a lot of truth in that statement. But, honestly, shouldn't it be! Especially if you are blessed enough to marry your soulmate. It was during these quiet moments that I began to loosen my grip and let her go. My social butterfly of a wife was now confined to a discolored body that was shutting down. My prayers suddenly changed to Lord, take her easy! Continue to allow no pain or discomfort to enter her body, as opposed to Lord, heal her to keep her here for me.

It's now Christmas Eve 2017! I'm feeling anxious and somewhat on edge this morning. This is fairly typical for me this time of the year. We celebrate Christmas in a big way at my parents' home on this day each year. While I enjoy celebrating the birth of our Lord and Saviour Christ Jesus, I'm not very comfortable in crowded situations. However, this year is very different. I'm very torn as to whether I should even attend or not. When Mary and I exchanged our "hey baby's" this morning, she barely opened her eyes and very faintly whispered. In hindsight, this would be the last communication that we would have. This is a clear indication that she may have just a day or less left to live. So, I need to make a decision as to whether to attend this celebration or stay put at my wife's side!

During this journey, so far up to this point by God's grace, I have been able to keep my promise to Mary concerning a couple of things. For starters, she asked me not to reveal to her mother her (Mary's) cancer diagnosis. Although I didn't fully understand her reasoning, I have kept that promise. Secondly, despite her condition, she wanted me to celebrate the holidays with our family as we always have. As trying as it was, I honored this request at Thanksgiving. Now I find myself praying about what to do on Christmas Eve.

As I was praying, the Holy Spirit brought to my remembrance the guidance that Hospice staff had recommended for such a time as this. Their recommendation was to go about your business as usual if possible. They implied, you may or may not want to be at your loved one's side when they take their last breath. Some people do, some people don't. We've had people who just briefly stepped away to use the restroom when their loved one passed. Unfortunately, these folks would oftentimes beat themselves up because they weren't present when their loved one passed. Hospice staff were adamant about me being kind to myself if I happened not to be present when Mary passed. If this were to be the case, the good Lord didn't want you to be present at that moment. I finally had peace in my heart to make a decision. I'm going to celebrate Christmas at my parents' home!

As much as I enjoyed the ride to my parents, the time spent at my parents was very emotional and draining. I rode with my daughter's family which had me seated next to my 9-month-old granddaughter in the backseat. She's a papa's girl so we had a blast during the trip. Once we arrived at my parents', I was approached by several family members (and rightfully so) enquiring about Mary's condition. It was in those moments of response that I realized Mary was going to be with Jesus on the day that we celebrate His birth. It made absolutely perfect sense! Years ago, Mary began stating the following on a frequent basis at Christmas time, "can you imagine being in Heaven on Christmas morning! With the angels singing and the trumpets blowing, celebrating the birth of Christ! Wow! What a sight that would be!" It appears that she may very well have a front row seat this Christmas!

The moment that was most special to me while at my parents was when my father held up and read a poster he had made in honor of Mary. It read like this, "if Mary were here, she would say take care of the elderly, the sick, the hungry, and the less fortunate. Everyone deserves to have a Merry Christmas; this is doing God's work! And as she left, she would turn and shout with a smiling face, Merry Christmas! I love you guys! To me, Mary was Christmas! I hope everyone has a "Mary" Christmas this year!" Whenever I reflect on that moment, tears stream down my face, just like they're doing now as I write this 5 years later.

Once arriving back at the Hospice facility, my daughter and I went inside to check on Mary. Hospice staff estimated that she would transition in the next 10-12 hours. With the midnight hour approaching, this meant she would probably pass somewhere between 10 a.m. and noon on Christmas morning. Just as Mary had instructed me to carry on during the holidays, she also instructed our son and daughter to do the same. So, they both planned to celebrate Christmas at home with their respective families that morning prior to coming to Hospice to celebrate with Mary and I at noon. With this new information, we still decided to go ahead and celebrate Christmas as planned. The only question remaining was will Mary be present in body or already celebrating in Heaven!

After my daughter had left, I settled into my bed attempting to get some rest. Surprisingly, my mind was not racing to and fro which is commonplace for me. I had this calmness about me that passes all understanding in this moment. I found myself thanking God for all He had done to see me through to this point. I thanked Him that Hospice staff still have not had to administer any pain medication to Mary. That she was resting peacefully. I thanked Him that arrangements had been made to properly honor and transport Mary's remains when her time arrives. On that note, at some point, I dozed off until a Hospice nurse awoke me at 5:30 a.m. She informed me that Mary could transition at any hour. That her breathing was somewhat laborous and they administered pain medication for the first time.

Once at Mary's side with a fresh cup of coffee, I began to caress her hands and gently kiss my baby on her cheek and forehead. I continuously told her how much I loved her and how much I was going to miss her. I found myself praying in the Spirit as each breath Mary took became shorter and more shallow. Mary's sister and cousin were present and would occasionally join beside me for support. As I was looking out the window on this dreary Christmas morning, I noticed a sudden opening in the clouds. What seemed like seconds later, rays of sunshine beamed through the open blinds lighting upon Mary's face. It was at this precise moment that Mary exhaled her last breath of life. It was as if heaven opened up to receive her spirit. Personally, I believe it was God's way of comforting me in my darkest moment of life. While I was relieved that she had been released from her cancer riddled body, I immediately slumped over her remains sobbing like never before!

CHAPTER THIRTEEN
MARY'S CORONATION DAY

For the record, my precious Mary transitioned from her earthly body to her heavenly home at 9:07 a.m. on Christmas Day 2017. Scripture tells us that for the Christian, our day of death is our coronation day! The day that indicates the ending of our earthly pilgrimage in a fallen world to the beginning of our presence before our Heavenly Father in an eternal heaven. It is the day that we are coronated into heaven by receiving a crown of righteousness from our Lord, Jesus! (2 Timothy 4:8, KJV) My precious Mary no longer has to imagine what it's like to be in heaven on Christmas morning. Yes indeed, she has a front row seat!

(above poem from an unknown author)

While the Hospice staff were respectfully preparing Mary's remains to be transported to our funeral home of choice, I made the two hardest phone calls I've ever made in my life. Notifying our children that their mom had gone to be with Jesus on Christmas morning was as emotionally trying as anything I've ever done in my life. I wished that I could just reach out and embrace them through the phone during our conversations. However, I knew that they would be arriving asap to spend some time with their mom prior to us celebrating Christmas at noon. There would be plenty of opportunities later in the day to share our emotions with one another. I believe in that moment I just wanted to physically hug the next closest living person/persons to Mary. Which of course would be our children.

Once the kids arrived with their families, we spent some individual as well as collective family time with Mary. Whether we realized it or not (probably not), it's important that each family member have their personal moments with Mary as needed to move forward in the grieving process. Due to each individual's uniqueness in relationship to Mary combined with each individual's temperament, it would be shortsighted to believe that we're all going to process her loss in the same way. I'm thankful that Hospice staff being cognizant of this fact allowed us to spend ample time with Mary. Once Mary's remains had been respectfully picked up for transport, we collectively relocated across the hall to begin our Christmas celebration.

I could never in a million years have imagined celebrating Christmas just a handful of hours after Mary dying. Especially in a room directly across from the room in which she passed at the Hospice facility. Having said that, here we are! The Hospice staff did an amazing job accommodating us for what turned out to be a unique celebration. For me personally, Mary's voice kept resonating within my being, speaking, "don't let what's going on with me interfere with or disrupt the holidays." This gave me cause to smile whereas previously it had saddened me. Fully aware that the shock of her passing hadn't even had a chance to begin to sink in, I realized through my reaction that the presence of the Lord was with me. That He would see me through the toughest of times. So, I chose to celebrate!

As my family and I were gathered around the Christmas tree opening presents, I paid special attention to our two grandchildren. Despite their ages of 17 and 9 months old, they were having a big time!

Or maybe it was because of their ages. Nonetheless, their exuberance carried over to all present as we joyously celebrated the birth of our Lord Jesus! At some point during our celebration, our daughter mentioned to me, "leave it to mom to work it out with God so she could participate in celebrating Christmas with both of her kids' families." You see, Mary had passed at 9:07 a.m. and was out of body to witness our kid's celebrations at 9:30 a.m. Our daughter also made a comment that put the moment in perspective. While her daughter was celebrating her first Christmas on earth, her mom had celebrated her last!

At some point during our Christmas celebration, the Director of the Hospice facility respectfully garnered my attention to have a conversation outside the room. She compassionately stated in a joyful tone of voice that my family and I were knocking the socks off of her and her staff. That they have never witnessed a family celebrating as we were after the loss of a loved one. I told her that it simply was the easiest and most practical thing to do. That her staff had went above and beyond to make this happen. From wrapping Christmas presents, to providing the room along with a meal to boot. It was a pretty easy decision to make. In that moment, we had no idea the positive rippling effect that had been initiated in the spiritual realm due to our celebration. I later was informed that testimony after testimony of our celebration had been given throughout Middle Tennessee. All I can say is that God in His sovereignty works in ways that are beneficial for His creation. He is the One who is worthy to receive all the glory, all the honor, and all the praise! In Jesus name, amen!

Once we concluded our celebration, we loaded the items that we had accumulated over the past 10 days into our respective vehicles. I personally went back inside and thanked the Hospice staff for being such a blessing during this most trying time. While driving home, I felt impressed in my spirit to notify Mary's primary day nurse at the Rehab facility of Mary's passing. This woman of God was not only a source of spiritual strength during Mary's 10 day stay in rehab, she provided companionship whenever her job allowed her to do so. I will forever be thankful for the way in which she chose to comfort Mary. She truly went above and beyond what her job required!

After arriving home and unloading my vehicle, I went to our bedroom and just collapsed on the bed. I was spent! I balled up in a fetal position and sobbed myself to sleep for several hours. Once awakening, it seemed as if everything was in a fog. Had the last 3 to 4 months really happened! Surely Mary couldn't have died! It was all a terrible nightmare! I'm sure once I awaken from this worstcase scenario everything will go back to normal! Unfortunately, not only was I wide awake but, this mindset would be something that I would struggle with for several months. At times, I felt like I was going crazy! I would later find out in counseling that feeling this way was normal. Yet, at some point, you have to establish what's called a "new normal." Again, I don't like it and it's just beginning!

With no time to spare, I needed to get dressed as my son, daughter and I are driving up to Kentucky to finalize funeral arrangements for Mary. While Mary had lived in the Nashville TN area for the past almost 40 years, prior to that she lived in the Gamaliel KY area from which she graduated high school. It would be one of her former classmates who would take care of her funeral arrangements. Due to these two locations being near and dear to her heart, she requested a Celebration of Life be held in the Middle TN area and her funeral followed by internment be held in Gamaliel KY. These two services would be held respectively on December 27th and 29th. Upon arrival, the three of us picked out a dark blue casket which featured a powder blue interior. This lighter interior would provide the perfect background to highlight the royal/sapphire blue dress in which Mary would be dressed. She loved this dress! It was the same dress that she wore to our daughter's wedding.

Upon arriving at the Celebration of Life facility, I was as nervous as I've ever been in my life. I purposely arrived there a couple of hours early to determine whether to have an open or closed casket. As previously noted, the entire right-side of Mary's face had turned a dark purple. She would not have been pleased if I allowed her to be viewed this way. Once entering the facility, I was graciously met by Mary's classmate who promptly introduced me to the facility's manager/owner. Once giving approval of the program provided for the service, they led me to the sanctuary to spend time with Mary prior to the service beginning. It was at this time I would make my decision concerning the open or closed casket issue.

As I slowly approached Mary's casket, I still couldn't believe that this was happening! That same foggy dreamlike state of mind that I had awaken to yesterday morning was still in full effect. I'll state again! I emphatically can't believe that this is happening! Nonetheless, as I find myself looking down at my Mary in her casket, I surprisingly burst out with tears of joy. She looked absolutely stunning! In my opinion, she looked like she would on her best day! The cosmetologist did an amazing job. Come to find out, the cosmetologist was the same person that always did Mary's hair. I will always be thankful for the care and service provided to Mary at this time. It was an easy decision to make. It would definitely be an open casket service!

Mary wanted her Celebration of Life service to be very casual filled with praise and worship for Jesus! To fulfill this request, a very dear friend of ours led the gathering by providing vocals accompanied by piano. He played several familiar worship songs that we had sang together throughout the past 3 to 4 decades. She loved when this particular friend led praise and worship at church. She often commented that it was because he played many of her favorites and that his singing voice didn't hurt things either. Again, Mary had quite the sense of humor. It was a job well done that evening. I'm sure that Mary was joining in with a smile as she looked down from heaven.

As for me, the least involved part of the service had been fulfilled. Now for the more involved and emotional aspect of the service. Mary's request was that after the reading of her obituary by funeral home staff, that I speak as the Lord leads. Once I'm finished, open up the floor to anyone in attendance to speak as they feel led. I was hoping to just speak for a couple of minutes while those in attendance would follow thus fulfilling the allotted time. However, this was not to be the case! I hesitate to say that what followed is unfortunate. I have learned throughout my Christian walk that the Lord orchestrates events in His timing for a reason. In His sovereignty, it was His will at this time for me to do the great majority of speaking.

What followed can only be best described as an out of body experience. I'm not a very social person and I certainly don't care for speaking in public. However, there have been numerous times during my Christian walk where the Lord has impressed upon me to do so. This would be one of those times. While it didn't feel that way, what happened with Mary unfolded very suddenly. Due to the short time-frame along with God's intervening times of healing, we as a family paused to notify several people of Mary's condition. So, the Lord wanted me to paint a picture with words if you will of Mary's journey. So, here we go!

As I began to speak, it's as if my spirit was detached standing alongside my body. I felt a comforting warmness throughout my body as if I was being coddled by my Heavenly Father. I believe that I was! As I observed the journey being illustrated with words, it was evident by the expressions of those in attendance that this testimony was resonating within. Honestly, I only remember bits and pieces of what was spoke. I do remember at some point my spirit reentered my body. In this moment, I became very emotional which prompted my son to step forward. He was strictly there to embrace and comfort his old man which was perfectly fine by me.

My father however at that point stood up to speak from where he was seated. He proceeded to tell a story about Mary. How he and my Uncle Charlie would pick on her. My Uncle Charlie had passed several years earlier. How he believed when Mary entered the pearly gates, that Uncle Charlie greeted her with, "it's about time "blondie", what took you so long?" They both called her "blondie" while telling dumb blonde jokes. It was a much-needed moment! I believe everyone in attendance erupted with laughter.

Once the service had concluded, I was approached by numerous people that I had encountered throughout my life. There was of course family, extended family, Mary's friends, our children's friends, and my friends. Frankly, I was overwhelmed by the respectfulness paid to Mary along with the outpouring of concern for my family and me. It was during this timeframe that several people commented, "the story you shared tied up some loose ends. I don't see how you did it!" I replied, "it wasn't me, praise the Lord." It was time to load up and head home. I was informed that numerous food items had been provided by those in attendance. Especially an abundance of fried chicken. This was such a blessing as we had enough food to last a few days. It was time to prepare for Mary's funeral.

Mary's funeral was to be exactly that, a traditional funeral. She had requested that a longtime friend of ours conduct her service. Mary and I considered this particular friend along with his wife our spiritual parents. His wife had gone to be with the Lord a couple of years prior to Mary. When I informed him of Mary's request, while he was honored, he was somewhat hesitant and reluctant. He replied, "oh Lord! This will be a tough one! However, I know that the Lord will see me through." Music and song would be provided by our same friend who led us in worship at Mary's Celebration of Life. Mary's obituary would be read by one of her former classmates. The funeral would be held at Mary's parents' home church in Gamaliel Ky. Her internment would follow thereafter in Gamaliel Cemetary. This is where her mother's family along with Mary's stepfather are buried.

I knew that this was going to be a very tough day. As expected, it was the toughest of days. Thankfully, I had no part to play in Mary's funeral other than to be present and accounted for. This allowed me to seek guidance and wisdom as best I could to be obedient in what the Lord had planned for me. Throughout Mary's funeral, I found myself reminiscing about our life together. From the very moment that we met in our church bowling league January 1981 until the moment she exhaled her last breath on Christmas morning 2017. It was during reliving some of these moments the Holy Spirit impressed upon me to take a big first step in moving forward. He instructed me to place my wedding band upon Mary's ring finger prior to her casket being closed.

At first, I didn't know what to think about this. Still being in a somewhat foggy state of mind, I needed to know that I was hearing clearly. I found myself asking, "are you sure Lord?" He immediately impressed upon my spirit, "you have fulfilled your commitment to Mary, till death do us part. Just as wearing your wedding band symbolizes the wholeness and ongoing commitment to Mary in marriage, by burying your wedding band with her, you'll be symbolizing the fulfillment and completion of that commitment in marriage." Despite my foggy state of mind, I now had crystal clear clarity concerning this request. Remember, God will never force us to do anything. He is a perfect gentleman! However, He knows what's best for us. It would be wise to be obedient to His promptings whether we fully understand or not! (Luke 5: 1-7, KJV)

With my instructions now in hand, I found myself primarily focused on Mary's remains for the rest of her service. I knew that at some point, the casket lid will be shut and I'll never lay eyes on her physical body again. This prompted tears from deep within to stream down my face. When this moment that I had been dreading arrived, my family and I approached Mary's casket. We both individually and collectively spent our final moments with her. It was the hardest moment that I've ever experienced in my life! Once the service concluded, we drove a short distance to the cemetery for a brief graveside prayer before the internment. This was sufficient due to the coldness of this December day. We then returned to the church to warmup, eat, and fellowship.

Mary's high school classmates went above and beyond providing a proper homegoing meal. From the décor to the food and beverages provided, they had transformed the dining area of the church for this occasion. I will always be thankful for the way in which they took our family in and respectfully honored Mary during this most trying time. Once the fellowship had concluded, we once again found ourselves loading up the SUV with an abundance of food along with multiple flower arrangements. Thankfully, my son and I were able to flag down my parents to take some of the food off our hands. There was plenty to go around.

Once my son and I left the church, we decided to stop by the cemetery along the way. For whatever reason, Mary's casket was not fully interred prior to us leaving the graveside prayer earlier that day. When we arrived at Mary's gravesite, we were greeted with a fully interred casket graced by a stunning temporary marker. The marker included Mary's most recent portrait in color along with her relevant information. I found it very comforting in this moment. We then retrieved a couple of flower arrangements from the SUV to place on her gravesite. Before departing, we visited some of Mary's relatives' gravesites as well.

While driving back home, my son asked me a pretty deep question. "Dad, why would God heal mom of brain cancer right after Thanksgiving, but then, allow her to die of lung cancer on Christmas Day?" I replied, "yeah, I know. I have given that some thought.

Honestly, for me personally, I don't think I'll ever understand why he didn't fully heal Mary's physical body. I mean He could have, He's God! However, I do know that your mom was not a happy camper being confined in an earthly body with limited ability to function. So, I've decided to accept the fact that it was the will of our Sovreign God for Mary to join Him on Christmas Day. I can say that I wasn't as ready to let her go around Thanksgiving as I was when she died on Christmas Day. So, I'll always be thankful for the extra weeks of time that we had together." My son, being a man of few words simply nodded in agreement.

CHAPTER FOURTEEN
A WHOLE NEW BALLGAME!!!
(In more ways than one)

It's now been just 2 seemingly long days since Mary's funeral. Even though it's been only 2 calendar days, the physical separation along with the now finalized tearing away of our souls continues to take its toll. While I realize that scientific studies suggest that a human soul weighs only 21 grams, I'm choosing to believe that it's more in line with 30 pounds. That's the amount of weight that I've lost during this journey. The physical separation aspect of grieving at this point is almost unbearable! I no longer have any options available to spend time physically with Mary. Despite the fact that I let Mary go, realizing how selfish it was for me to hold onto her in any condition; I'm now finding out that this doesn't alleviate the pain that I now experience. This side of death really is a whole new ballgame! Speaking of ballgames, my son just alerted me it's time to go watch the Titans!

As indicated earlier, we've had TN Titans season tickets for several years. The majority of the time my son and I would attend while Mary and my daughter would occasionally fill in. So, this was a very familiar and comforting environment for my son and me to be in. However, today would be an indication of how daily and routine things in life are affected while one is grieving. Some of these changes are positive and help assist in healing and moving forward while some not so much! The not so much aspect experienced today would be the total lack of tolerance for people being inconsiderate, disrespectful, and rude.

When a father and his 2 adult sons broke line while entering the stadium, this prompted my son to confront them verbally. Their reaction being nonapologetic, prompted me to want to reach out and touch someone in a not so neighborly way. While words continued to be exchanged, thankfully, the father realized he best shut his youngest son's mouth before someone shut it for him. There were a lot of angry people they had cut in front of who were willing to do this. The father eventually admitted their wrongdoing and offered to let my son and me in front of them. We refused stating that they needed to go to the back of the line. They chose to stay put which was not surprising.

As we worked our way to our seats, my son apologized for his actions. I told him he didn't have anything to apologize for. While his actions were warranted, I was caught off guard by his tone of voice and body language. This was out of character for him. I was also surprised by the impulse I had to physically restrain someone. I hadn't experienced that feeling since my military days nearly 40 years ago. I realized in that moment, how Mary's death had begun to impact our lives as we grieved her passing. While I became less patient and tolerable with people in these types of scenarios, my compassion grew for people whose situations warranted it.

Now for the positive aspects experienced today. Sports have always played a big part in my life. My father officiated both high school and college junior varsity sports throughout my childhood. Being the oldest of 5 children, I had the privilege of accompanying him to several games. Due to this, I've always enjoyed watching sports. Whether on tv or live and in person as I find myself doing in this very moment. Having my son here with me makes it even more special. As the game progressed, I find myself at times getting overwhelmed with emotion combined with periods of uncontrollable sobbing. Sometimes, these emotions were triggered while reminiscing about Mary but occasionally would just come out of nowhere. I would later find out in grief counseling that these unexpected outbursts of emotion are known as "ambush grief". Again, I don't like it and it's just the beginning!

Once the game had ended, my son and I chose to hang around and enjoy the celebration. The Titans had beaten the Jaguars which earned them a berth in the playoffs at Kansas City the following Saturday. This prompted me to check online to see if any tickets were available for this game. Amazingly, there were 4 front row seats available on the 20-yard line at face value. I immediately purchased them with the intent of my son along with 2 other fortunate Titans fans attending the game. As my son and I were discussing who to ask to join us for the trip, I suddenly smelled Mary's perfume. At this point, there was no one standing near us! Along with the fact that her perfume was special order, made this moment even more intriguing. On this note, we left the stadium pretty emotional and somewhat puzzled!

With this being New Years's Eve, we headed back to my son's house to rest up and prepare for a small celebration that evening.
He and his wife were having a couple over to celebrate New Year's with us. The husband of this particular couple along with a mutual friend of his and my sons would join us in attending the game in Kansas City. Now that we had all the particulars sorted out for that trip, I just settled in for the evening mainly spending time with my grandson. Once the midnight hour had come and gone ringing in a New Year, I promptly retired to my bedroom hoping to get some quality sleep.

Once saying my prayers and laying comfortably in bed, I had numerous thoughts racing through my mind. The thought that I kept entertaining was how was it possible that I smelled Mary's perfume at the ballgame! It just didn't make any sense! After being entertained out on that particular thought, I began to think about the week ahead. For the time being, I would spend Thursday night thru Monday morning at my son's, while spending Monday morning thru Thursday night at my daughter's. My daughter had suggested that we attend a grief counseling group that met at our church on Thursday nights. They would be starting a new 13week cycle this Thursday, January 5, 2018. While still somewhat reluctant to attend (mainly due to a group setting), I told her I would based on my positive experience with the grief counselor from Oncology.

Once my daughter and I arrived at the grief meeting, we promptly found 2 seats to fill at the rectangular shaped table and chair setting. This type setting allowed everyone in attendance to have visual contact with those attending. As soon as we were seated, one of the facilitators of the group handed us individual forms to provide our relevant information. Honestly, I'm still foggy minded as I reflect back on that first night. However, I do remember some statements and comments made either directly or indirectly that continue to be foundational in my life.

The meeting was scheduled to be conducted during a 2-hour timeframe. This would consist of a 45-minute video followed by group discussion concluding with prayer. While watching the video, I was immediately drawn into the content being discussed. The hosts narrating the video began to list numerous things that you may or may not be experiencing since the death of your loved one. Having experienced a handful of these things, they had my undivided attention. At that point in time, I knew that my daughter and I had come to the right place.

As the session continued, whether by means of video or group discussion, I received the answers to some questions that I had. I learned that the sudden outbursts of uncontrollable sobbing and emotion are referred to as "ambush grief." That this is to be expected and considered normal behavior at this time. That during your grief journey you'll experience what are referred to as "miracle moments." Moments where God supernaturally steps into time to comfort you along this path. Moments such as smelling your wife's perfume at a ballgame. During this time, you may feel as if you've lost your mind and are going crazy. As if you're the guest of honor living out your worst nightmare. That it's all a bad dream! That surely, you'll awaken to how things were before returning to normal – unfortunately, or fortunately, depending on your perspective.....welcome to the first step of finding your "new normal!"

Once the session concluded, an older gentleman sitting next to me introduced himself. His wife had passed a couple of years prior and he had already attended 2 cycles (26 weeks) of this program. He stated very clearly, "I know you have a relationship with the Lord! However, you're going to have to lean in and depend on Him like you never have before in your life to properly heal from your loss! I tried to navigate this journey on my own and fell flat on my face! That's why I'm here now!" I told him that I appreciated his guidance and looked forward to speaking further with him at future sessions.

When my daughter and I were leaving the session, we were approached by the facilitator who had provided the forms for us to fill out. She simply stated, "I don't know what it is about you two, but ya'll are my kind of people!" I'm sure that we acknowledged her, but honestly, I don't remember. However, I do remember leaving with a sense of direction that had previously been absent. While I was obviously still in shock and experiencing that deep, continuous gut-wrenching pain, this sense of direction that I had inherited tonight provided me with a certain comfort. A comfort that somehow, someway provided a deep peace within my spirit that help offset some of the pain that I was experiencing. Again, I took this as confirmation that my daughter and I had come to the right place!

Due to the fact that our Kansas City trip began the following day, I decided to spend the night at my home as opposed to my son's home. I knew that it was going to be very challenging but this would allow me to pack and prepare for our trip. As I entered my home, I was immediately greeted by the Christmas tree and various decorations that I had put on display. This had been done in hopeful anticipation of Mary being healed, thus coming home to a beautifully decorated home to celebrate Christmas. However, this was simply not to be the case!

As I was packing for the trip, moment by moment, the realization of Mary dying began to bombard every aspect of my being. Suddenly, I found myself slumped on the floor in the living room underneath our family portrait. As tears streamed down my face, I began to plead my case to God, "how could you allow this to happen! Mary didn't deserve this! I don't deserve this! My kids don't deserve this, and on and on! I began to quote God's word to Him as if He didn't know it! I was angry, hurt, lonely, but most of all disappointed that my God whom I love and serve had dropped the ball thwarting my plans! This is not what's best for me, Lord!"

As I continued to lay slumped on the floor, attempting to somewhat compose myself, that still, small voice that resides within began to gently speak to me, "Mickey! I know you're hurting son! Believe me! I can more than identify and feel what you're experiencing! Remember, I created man in my image! Despite me being God of all creation, people have a tendency to forget that I experience the same emotions and feelings as my crown of creation does. However, you must remember who I am and respect My sovereignty! While it endears Me that you choose to seek Me out first and foremost with your pleas, I must remind you that it's My plans and purposes that will prevail, not yours! While you may think you know what's best for you and your family, that's simply not true and you know that."

"As I reminded Job of old, I must now remind you! Who are you that questions my wisdom with such ignorant words? Brace yourself like a man, because I have some questions for you, and you must answer them. Where were you when I laid the foundations of the earth? Tell me, if you know so much. Who determined its dimensions and stretched out the surveying line? What supports its foundations, and who laid its cornerstone as the morning stars sang together and all the angels shouted for joy? Do you still want to argue with the Almighty? You are God's critic, but do you have the answers?" (Job 38: 1-7 & 40: 1-2, NLT)

Like Job of old, I had cried uncle by humbling myself and repenting long before He finished reminding me of who He was, is, and will always be! How foolish I had been to question God's sovereign plans for my family and me! Once I had managed to reposition myself now sitting upright as opposed to laying on the floor, the Lord continued to minister to me. "Mickey! Do you really think that I would allow something so painful to impact your life without there being beneficial consequences? Of course, a lot of this depends on you! Unfortunately, a number of my children when faced with adverse circumstances choose to allow Satan to sift through them as fine wheat. They allow him to dispose them of their faith in Me!" (Luke 22: 31 NLT)

"If you choose! I have plans that will prosper you exceedingly and abundantly above anything that you can ask for or imagine! I will be able to utilize you in My kingdom in ways that you never dreamed of! Remember, the road that I have chosen for you will be very difficult to navigate. Especially, if you choose to do so alone! That's why I orchestrated for you to sit next to the gentleman tonight (at Griefshare) who shared his journey with you. He attempted to navigate this journey on his own and failed miserably! While it may appear in a fallen world that I'm no longer sovereign and in control, don't believe this lie!"

"You must be mindful that I was, am, and always will be a God of freewill! I will always provide my children with the necessary information (My Holy Word, testimonies) required to always make the best decision. To always do as they should, not as they ought!
That's why I provided you with this man's testimony! Now you have a choice to make! Are you going to solo it as you occasionally choose to handle things without Me? Are you going to somewhat include Me as you oftentimes do? Or, are you going to fully allow Me to be in control which you seldom do? It's totally up to you, Mickey!" Seeing how I had already pulled a "Job"! I found myself saying, "yes, Lord! I desire for you to take the lead and be fully in control."

Now that I have a better understanding of who God is, the Holy Spirit brought a couple of things to my remembrance. The first and most recent being what the gentleman at Griefshare had stated. How I'm going to have to lean into God, allowing Him to take charge and be in complete and total control to properly heal. I've heard that message twice tonight, loud and clear! The second being, 20 plus years ago while involved with youth group at church. We had a guestspeaker one evening who proceeded to tell us about 3 different categories of people.

The 3 categories that people fall into when making decisions in life. The first category are geniuses. Geniuses are people who exercise wisdom by learning from other people's mistakes. For instance, if I had adhered to and learned from Job's experience, I would have been considered a genius by choosing not to question God's sovereignty. However, since I did question God's sovereignty. I now fall into the second category of people, which are smart people. Most of us tend to fall into this category when making decisions in life. We have to learn from and experience the mistakes that we've made as opposed to learning from other people's mistakes. Unfortunately, if you don't learn from your mistakes you fall into the third and final category as being stupid or foolish. People in this category continue to make the same mistakes continuously without ever learning. I found myself hoping to be a genius from this point forward in the situation I found myself in. Realizing my previous track record, I knew that I would have to lean into and depend on the Lord like never before!

Now that we're finally on the road to Kansas City.....despite my broken condition, I'm as excited as I've been in some time! I'm really looking forward to watching a football game at Arrowhead Stadium. The Lord had already impressed upon my heart that this trip would be about much more than a football game. With that in mind, what a blessing it is to have front row seats for a playoff game at what is considered to be the loudest stadium in the NFL. Along with the Titans participating....this is going to be awesome!!!

As we drive towards St. Louis working our way to Kansas City, we pass along an area that's very familiar to me. Mary's stepdad and brother owned campers on Lake Barkley in the Cadiz KY area. Early on in our marriage, we would spend some weekends there in the summer. While I'm not much for fishing, I really enjoyed being on the water with family. It was at that moment, I realized that this trip would be a continuation of the grieving process. By taking me down memory lane, the Lord was revealing to me this is how you lean into grieving. Despite how painful it may be at times. With My help! You need to entertain and experience the memories that come your way. If you choose to do so! This will be of great assistance in your healing process. If you choose not to! You'll fall flat on your face as the gentleman you met in Griefshare did. The choice is yours!

Once arriving at Arrowhead Stadium, what a sight! The stadium itself is literally encompassed by what seems like miles and miles of concrete parking area. We were on the lookout for a Titan's speck of blue in the midst of a Chief's sea of red! The local sports radio station from Nashville were onsite in Kansas City broadcasting the game. With our target in sight, we promptly found a parking space and congregated with approximately 5,000 Titans fans in attendance. During this time, we met the owner of the Titans who very graciously took photos with us along with several others in attendance. We couldn't have asked for a better start to our day!

After entering the stadium and making our way to our seats, the Lord impressed upon me to just look around and take in the view. He whispered, "it's not happenstance that you find yourself seated in the front row! I orchestrated for you along with others in attendance today for your respective paths to cross. Whether it's the front row or the last row you find yourself in, remember, I'm always with you! I will never leave you or forsake you! Where I call you to be will always be the safest place for you because it's in My will! Some of your encounters today will be pleasant, while others not so much! However, this is typical in a fallen world. It's important for you to remember and understand that my ways and thoughts are much higher than yours. I'll be accomplishing much more in My Kingdom today than you could ever think or imagine. Enjoy the day my child!"

Once the conversation with my Heavenly Father had concluded, it was time for my first encounter of the day. Thankfully, we had aisle seats 1-4 in our row. This made it very convenient to exit for food and restroom breaks. I chose to sit in seat number 4. Normally, I would sit in aisle seat 1. However, the Lord had impressed upon me to sit next to whoever would in seat number 5. While personally I didn't care for this, this would be a big first step in me choosing to follow God's lead as opposed to me flying solo. I didn't want this journey to be any more painful and treacherous than it already was.

My first encounter of the day ended up being with a gentleman around 60 years of age (such as myself) who sit in seat 7 as opposed to seat 5. Whoever was sitting in seats 5 & 6 had not arrived yet. With us being dressed in Titan blue, this gentleman inquired as to how we ended up with the seats we had. I told him that they were available on Ticketmaster for face value. My response seemed to puzzle him. He somewhat muttered under his breath that he hoped that they were okay. He informed me that the regular occupants of these seats had been sitting here for 25 plus years. That it was unlike them to not be in attendance.

Especially for a playoff game. I told him that I would be praying that they're fine. He simply nodded in agreement. On that note, we shook hands, both hoping for a well officiated ballgame with each other hoping our individual team wins. This encounter was very pleasant and would continue to be so. The next encounter, not so much!

The occupants of seats 5 & 6 turned out to be not my favorite kind of people! They were brothers approximately 35 to 40 years of age in the neighborhood of my son's age. While I don't condone drunken behavior, I certainly have no issue with someone enjoying themselves. Especially at a playoff game! Again! I have no problem with a certain amount of "ribbing" from fans of the opposing team. Especially in their home stadium. This is to be somewhat expected. However, I will not tolerate 2 drunken idiots in my face calling me every profane name under the sun. Suddenly, I find myself in the same situation as the week before at the Titans game. I wanted to reach out and touch someone in a not so neighborly way. By the grace of God, I find myself calmly but yet firmly telling these guys to knock it off or I'll get security. Thankfully, my new found friend in seat 7 convinced these guys to settle down or he would call security.

Now, finally the game starts! While of course I wanted the Titans to win the game, I was simply very thankful that my son and I were enjoying ourselves despite Mary's recent death. At the moment, it's good that I have this perspective because the Titans are getting beat 21 to 3 at halftime. While most people had cleared out due to halftime, I suddenly just burst out sobbing uncontrollably.

That dreaded "ambush grief" strikes again! I immediately feel a comforting hand on my shoulder. It's my new friend from seat number 7. He smilingly states, "it's okay man! I know ya'll are getting beat 21 to 3 but it's just a ballgame!" With a smile, I inform him that my wife of 35 plus years died this past Christmas morning. That's why I'm crying!

He proceeded to tell me how sorry he was for my loss. How he's currently been married for a similar length of time. That he can't imagine what kind of shape he would be in under a circumstance such as this. He apologized for me having to put up with the drunken fans in seats 5 & 6. However, fortunately for us, those 2 seats belong to a corporation. These 2 guys will rotate out with 2 other coworkers for the 2nd half. So, we're done with those guys! He said it had been his experience throughout the years that the other people in the corporation's rotation had been very pleasant people. As the 2nd half began, he again stated that he was sorry for my loss.

Being a Titans fan, the 2nd half could not have been scripted any better! The Titans outscored the Chiefs 19 to 0, winning the game in thrilling come from behind fashion. The final score being 22 to 21! Once the final whistle had sounded, my new found friend in seat number 7 stopped by to offer his congratulations. He further stated that I hope you guys beat the Patriots. That he really didn't care for them. He concluded this conversation by once again offering his condolences concerning Mary's death. That he and his family would continue to lift my family and me up in prayer. I found myself being very thankful that God chose for our paths to cross today.

While the nearly 75,000 disgruntled Chiefs fans exited the stadium, the Titans fans in attendance made their way to the front row in each section. When all is said and done, Titans fans had encircled the perimeter of the playing field. It was an awesome sight to see! It was at this time that I smelled Mary's perfume for now a second time! Remember, the first time being at the Titans game in Nashville the previous week! The difference being this time, I'm fully aware that this is God providing another "miracle moment" to assist in comforting me. Whereas previously, being unaware of such moments. It left me puzzled! Again, this is confirmation that counseling would be necessary to assist in navigating this journey.

For the next hour or so, we were allowed to celebrate with the Titans players themselves! The players individually made their way around the perimeter of the field. They took time to shake hands and chat with each fan individually. While all this was happening, my phone starting "blowing up" with text messages. Apparently, my son and I were on live tv being aired on ESPN. This prompted us to immediately locate the live cameras thus proceeding to make fools of ourselves by behaving "fanatically". It was at this time stadium security encouraged those remaining in attendance to exit the stadium.

Once satisfying our appetites with assorted smoked pork products at a local bar-be-que establishment (which by the way was overrun with Titans fans), we headed back home towards Nashville. The plan was for my son to drive for 3 ½ hours to St. Louis, with me then driving the remaining 5 hours home. With my son driving, this afforded me the opportunity to rest as needed. As we work our way eastbound on I-70, the Holy Spirit begins to bring some things to my remembrance.

In December 1981, approximately 3 ½ months prior to Mary and I marrying, we had actually drove from Kansas City to Nashville. The company who I was working for at the time needed someone to fly to Kansas City and drive a company car back to Nashville. With the company paying for our airfare along with other traveling expenses, I volunteered. This would be our first road trip of many to come over the next 36 years. Honestly, I had forgotten about this trip! Maybe because it was mainly work related. I'm not sure. Despite the reason, the Holy Spirit continued to take me down memory lane. While doing so, He imparted into my spirit that this would be commonplace for the remainder of the year. This "It's A Wonderful Life" journey will be a vital part in your Heavenly Father's plan for your healing. So, with the hope that we have in Jesus! (1 Thessalonians 4:13) Let the grieving continue.......

CHAPTER FIFTEEN
GOOD GRIEF???

This level of grief is unlike any that I've ever experienced in my life. In the scheme of things, it should be! When Mary died, in essence, the rest of my life that was to be died as well. All of our hopes, dreams, and plans from here on out had suddenly vanished! I had incurred other losses in my life, but none as significant as a spouse. When a spouse dies, you don't just lose a wife as is the case with me. You lose a soulmate, helpmate, prayer partner, best friend, travelling companion, lover, confidant, encourager and the list goes on and on. Realizing what I've lost, I need help! I need a plan!! I need God!!!

During this journey, God utilized several people to minister to me both prior to and after Mary's death. While I will always be thankful for everyone who played a part in this process, the one who impacted me most was a "Chaplain" who visited us at the hospital. It was a one-time random visit which lasted 30 – 45 minutes. I don't remember his name and haven't seen or heard from him since! The visit occurred on the afternoon of December 1, 2017. The day in which Mary had suffered her 3rd stroke earlier that morning. She obviously wasn't doing very well, neither was I for that matter.

Once he entered the room, he simply introduced himself as a "Chaplain" who was passing through. That he was sent to minister which in turn would provide comfort for us. With Mary being asleep, he proceeded to tell me his testimony. How unfortunately for him (which turns out to be fortunate for me), he found himself in a similar situation a couple of years ago. How despite having a strong faith and continually praying for his wife to be healed. She eventually succumbed to a short battle with cancer. How he struggled with why God would allow this to happen. How the Holy Spirit had impressed upon him to accept this cup that God had allowed, as opposed to fighting it. He had my undivided attention.

He proceeded to share with me what God had impressed upon him during his similar experience. He stated, "what I'm about to tell you will be hard for you to hear. However, just as it was for me, it will be what's best in providing some comfort for you as well. You're probably sitting here worrying about your wife dying. The pain that she's enduring. How your life is going to be without her.

Due to these concerns, you're probably experiencing that knot in the pit of your stomach. If this is you, this makes you normal! God created us with emotions. These are the emotions you should be experiencing! Remember, our Lord Jesus in the Garden of Gethsemane experienced grief and distress to the point of death!" (Matthew 26: 37-38, NASB)

"It's important to remember, when we experience these emotions (just as Jesus did), it doesn't indicate a lack of faith. On the contrary! It suggests that "because of your faith", you're struggling with a cup that God has allowed to be handed to you. You struggle because you realize that you can't change or survive this on your own! Sadly, it was my mindset prior to my wife's death that I was somewhat bulletproof to the tragedies in life. God never promised us a perfect life with sunshine and rainbows every moment of our lives. Just ask John the Baptist who was beheaded. Thankfully, what He promised is that He would be with us in every moment, of every circumstance, that we will face in this fallen world! It's of the upmost importance that you have a plan going forward that includes God!!!" I thanked him for his encouragement as he ended his visit in prayer.

I've now been on this "grief train" for a couple of months. As I sit at home drinking coffee, I reflect back over the past several months: How God orchestrated people (such as the "Chaplain") to come into my life; People who have been instrumental in the implementation of the "grief plan" now in place. My daughter and I continue to attend the weekly Thursday night Griefshare sessions at church. In addition to this, I see an individual grief counselor biweekly. The Hospice facility in which Mary resided provides a free year of counseling for family members.

Despite taking advantage of these resources, I continue to be a "hot mess" most of the time. I continue to have nightmares along with panic attacks. Panic attacks are something I've dealt with over the years from military induced trauma; however, since Mary died, they occur more frequently and are more intense, even though the two events happened decades apart. They trigger one another causing more intense attacks. As difficult as my current condition is, this is considered to be "normal" behavior considering the circumstance. While reminding myself of this reality provides me some much-needed comfort, the pain both mentally and physically continue to be exhausting. I have never experienced fatigue like this in my life!

Based on recommendations through counseling, it would be wise to have a complete physical examination conducted. When losing a spouse to a disease or medical condition, your mind will usually play tricks on you, especially concerning your health! This is what brings me to my primary care physician today. He has been my doctor for 23 years now. He usually stays on me about losing weight. Today would be different!

After entering his office and looking up from my chart, his expression said it all! Surprisingly, he was speechless for what seemed like several minutes but in reality, was just several seconds. He finally managed to squeak out, "Michael, what's going on with you?"

I proceeded to tell him about Mary's illness which led to her eventual death. While consoling me (which is atypical), he proceeded to conduct his examination. Thankfully, when the examination had concluded. My overall physical health was better than it had been in years. And, for the first time in our acquaintanceship, he spoke the words I'd been longing to hear. He stated, "you need to gain some weight! You look unhealthy!" Thank you, Jesus!

Receiving a clean bill of health (physically anyway), gave me a peace of mind that had been missing. I now realized that all I'm experiencing is grief related. This encouraged me to dig in even closer to God. I wish I could say that I've been a genius to this point in dealing with my grieving; however, that would be a lie! But! To be fair and kind to myself (which is highly recommended during this time), I am progressing! Unfortunately, at times, I choose to drink more and more often than I normally would in the past. I've arrived at a very critical juncture in my grief journey. I must choose to exercise Godly wisdom; for this could become a very slippery slope, one in which I didn't want to slide back down. Fortunately, by His grace, I stop drinking!

In what I consider to be my darkest moment on this journey. I find myself sitting on the bench in our walk-in shower. Due to our age, Mary and I had decided to remove our garden tub and install a walk-in shower to better accommodate us. Unfortunately, she never had the opportunity to utilize it. Oftentimes, I would find myself sitting fully clothed, in the shower thinking about what might have been. While I never entertained the thought of suicide; I occasionally thought it wouldn't be so bad if the Lord would just take me on home either. In this darkest of moments, I needed a sign! I needed another "miracle moment".

As I continue to sit in the shower, sobbing uncontrollably, there are numerous memories racing through my mind. Despite most of them being positive, they seem to heighten my pain! At this point, I'm pleading with God to show me a sign. I begin to shout, "I know you're there, Lord! I know you'll never leave me or forsake me! But, I'm in a really bad way, Lord! I need confirmation!" At that moment, that still, small voice within whispered, "it's right in front of you Mickey!" With my head slumped down. I noticed at the base of the wall just slightly above the floor, a beautiful rainbow. Mary loved rainbows! Once again! God had provided another "miracle moment" to comfort me when I needed it most!

I've now been on the "grief train" for approximately 5 months. While the hard work is beginning to pay off, in some ways, at times the journey seems to be getting worse. Some hard truths pertaining to grief are beginning to sink in, such as life will never be the same that it was prior to your loved one dying. It's not possible, but there will be life! On the upside, you become more aware that it's possible for both pain and peace to coexist. You begin to understand that the foggy mindedness (shock) that you're experiencing is an intrinsic cocoon of protection that God has provided; that as this shock continues to dissipate, it's God's way of measuring out to you what you can handle. (1 Corinthians 10: 13, NLT)

I now find myself being of assistance in the Griefshare program at church. The Lord impressed on my heart to "buddy up" with men going through a similar circumstance as I am. Despite us being widowers around the same age, there are numerous factors that come into play on your individual grief journey. While it would be unwise to compare one another's journey; I find myself being thankful in certain respects. I'm thankful that I'm retired. I couldn't imagine going through this while working. Also, while it was no "cakewalk", I find myself being thankful that Mary and I had time beforehand as opposed to her dying suddenly.

As this "grief train" continues, I find myself with a new found hope that had previously been missing. Where at one point, I didn't know if I would survive this journey, I am gaining traction and stronger on my feet as I acclimate to my "new normal!" While I will never understand the timing in which Mary died; I am no longer angry, having accepted the fact that it was within God's will. I'm finally at a place in my life where peace outweighs the pain that continues to coexist. In conclusion, I now fully understand, when you grieve with the hope we have in Christ, that God truly shows Himself strongest in broken places, even WHEN THE ANSWER IS NO!!!